"BUDDHISM AND OTHER SUCH RUBBISH!"

GAVIN WEBSTER

Typeset in Caroni

Editing, design, typesetting and publishing by UK Book Publishing

www.ukbookpublishing.com

ISBN: 978-1-914195-99-0

TO ALL PEOPLE WHO LIKE TO TALK BUT ESPECIALLY
TO ALI AND DEVON WHO TALK AND TALK AND TALK

CONTENTS

INTRODUCTION

There are those who won't like this book and it's those who have no sense of humour. Simple as that. It's not arrogance or me trying to wind you up as a reader, but a simple fact. Humour, or at least a decent attempt at humour is good, I'll always give support to someone who tries to attempt a bit of humour even if it doesn't quite land. I appreciate there are people who try it and it's excruciating, but if someone has a good shot at it, I'll always feel entertained. Maybe it's an honour amongst thieves because I'm in the humour business but a half decent comedian in my eyes is much better than a half decent artist or a half decent actor or screenwriter. Honestly, it's funny, read on!

Oh yes I'm well aware of the disclaimers from the naysayers – 'Listen, mate, no one likes a laugh more than me but....' Watch out for that lot, the 'no one likes a laugh more than me brigade' are the people who find it very difficult to ever kick back and have a laugh and go out of their way to be po-faced about absolutely anything and everything, it's not just something you've said that they don't like, believe you me. The humourless will always be humourless, but they go out of their way to tell you that they normally have a ball, it's just you that's making them have a face like a smacked arse. Don't listen to them; they're full of misery. 'That's not funny' is a phrase I like as well. Enunciating the beautiful chemical reaction of laughter into words, but doing the opposite by disproving it through a three-word riposte without any evidence or workings out to go with it like they were God or Judge Dredd or something. They are, in their own overblown egotistical eyes, the arbiters of laughter. These people tend, a lot of the time, to work full time in education – 'putting a biscuit on your head isn't funny, Rebecca, put it back in your lunch box and we can all start learning again.'

Of course, you're very welcome to not like my first attempt at a book; to be honest if you've come this far, you're either in the shop reading it or you're having a sneaky peek on the bus home and if so thanks for the purchase. I was going to write 'kerching' like the noise of an old fashioned till putting into words a sound which some folk do to signify that they've managed to acquire some easy money from dumb punters due to them being class or a bit of a maverick. I suppose I'm toying with doing this to maybe put people off that I don't like from buying the book, so by being as reprehensible and annoying as possible early doors and without irony I can lose a few misery guts readers and really serious berks, but I won't do that – you might be a complete berk or maybe not, maybe you're easily the funniest person in your street; the trouble is, loads of people think that they are that, even the 'no one likes a laugh more than me' platoon.

In this country we all think we've got a sense of humour; some people think theirs is too nuanced or too sophisticated for other people to get it or that others don't understand their irony or their sarcasm, but in general the British people as individuals like to think that they're funny and love to get laughs and recognition of their great wit and playful patter. To insult someone in this country by telling them that they're humourless or have not one funny bone in their body or have never said anything funny in their life really cuts like a knife. Look at Americans wanting to always be cool, or Australians wanting to be beach-ready with a six pack, or a Canadian ready at all times to be able to live outdoors off natural resources for a month, and then look at the Brits. What are we ready for? We're ready to say something 'funny'. Whether we're from rural Lincolnshire or Methil in Fife, we as an island people always like to think we've got a great sense of humour. Anyone who hasn't got any kind of sense of humour in this country really isn't of any use to anyone. You could be shit at your job, but if you're a laugh you're still in the game if you're British. It's one of the few things I'm still proud of in this increasingly fractionated and devolved country.

It's with that where you can insult me if you want. Get in touch with me on @Thegavinwebster on twitter and say something like 'it's not the lack of accurate facts or the fact that it doesn't follow a pattern or a story arc, it's not that it's too wordy or not wordy enough, the reason why I don't like the book is because it's NOT FUNNY! I'll be devastated. You'd hurt me the most if you said something like that. Mind you, that might be more than 280 characters!

Gavin Webster stand-up comedian 2020 in between lockdowns

MY OPENING DISCLAIMER

Hello, my name is Gavin Webster, I'm a stand-up comedian. I was a lot of things before I landed this ridiculous occupation, but all of those things were just temporary. I could list all of them with a bit of an editorial attached, but this isn't my autobiography. That won't take place for a long time, if ever. Whatever I do with the time I've got left on this Earth, be it long or short, I'll always be a stand-up comedian. That was my thing. I hope in the future when I'm long gone people might say 'the feller in this house was a stand-up comedian' or 'do you know my grandad bought this car when he was young from an old feller who was, believe it or not, one of those a stand-up comedians' — you get the idea. I am a stand-up comedian, I do it because I sort of enjoy it. I certainly don't dread every day and I can honestly say hand on heart, I managed to, against the odds, alleviate that 'Monday morning feeling', in fact I might have never really suffered from that since I took up stand-up comedy full time. There's people that would kill to stop that feeling and I managed it; it's still my greatest personal achievement in all honesty.

It wasn't what I was born to do though, you must understand, I certainly don't see it that way. I don't know about you but I hate that phrase, I wasn't built by the good lord himself (most people assume that he's a man) to tell funny stories in front of audiences, but I learnt how to do it whilst realising that I've an understanding and an interest about the world around us, coupled with the fortunate quirk of having a natural flair for words, plays on words, spoonerisms, anecdotes that are meant to be ironic, anecdotes that aren't, contradictory sentences, good old fashioned daftness and nonsense, as well as soliloquys and non sequiturs, and of course perfect lucid sense in between all of these flights of fancy to punctuate it all. I'm ironic, sardonic, cruel and aggressive in just the right dose, also I'm charming and likeable at the appropriate times as well without being oily or seedy like some blokes. Well at least I think I am anyway! I make a living from it and have done so full time since the end of 1997.

I'm of my time. I haven't got a funny face so I wouldn't have fit in with the variety club era, I'm not from a music hall family that benefited greatly 100 years ago from nepotism. I don't look good in a suit and can't tell 'two fellers talking' type of patter, so I may not have cut it 50 years ago in the dreaded working men's clubs; also I wasn't Oxbridge enough to be a face on the London alternative circuit in the 80s, and nowadays I do look a lot of times like some sort of anachronism in the post-woke, anything goes however I'm offended era where we find ourselves now. I'm becoming out of touch but that's just one of those things. At the time of writing I feel that us 90s comics are writing our own obituaries; however, I'm not one of those who laments that, if I end up delivering pizzas or working in a DIY store because of the need for lid lifting bisexual, trivial camp stories with a Fear And Loathing In Las Vegas narrative as well as ultra right-on comics and to balance it out uber right wing tell it like it is performers rather than a Geordie telling good jokes that he's written himself then so be it, I had my time.

The great Malcolm Macdonald (ask your dad) would have been able to play football today at the top level no problem and The Small Faces would have been a chart phenomenon with their records in these times, and of course impresarios of today know this, they'll deny it but they know it. What they're trying and indeed needing to do is make it look like that there's sensations coming over the hill every year even better than the sensations that came before them, when in fact in terms of cultural renaissance for the jet age, things peaked quite a while ago. Capitalism eats itself as it goes and of course showbusiness (the clue is in the business bit) is not immune from that.

What this book is though is honest. It's all I can give and that's to be as sincere as I can. Mind you, some of it might be made up, I'm allowed that privilege. And you're allowed to disagree, you're allowed to be offended and affronted that I get so many things wrong because everyone is a critic these days, that's your right as a reader.

Feel privileged that you heard a point of view from a certain time, that's how I feel when I read stuff. From Chaucer to Samuel Pepys to Anne Frank to some penis like Tony Parsons, it's always great to see what someone felt in a certain time be it a time of great hope or a time of misery, whether they're pointing out a gross injustice in society like Dickens or someone describing a great sporting occasion with the social backdrop like Hugh McIlvanney. Hopefully in 100 years' time this book will seem ridiculous in its world view; it would be depressing if it all rang true and we had never moved on as a society. It's there though, frozen in time, the 50 year old comedian at his wits' end about people and their lack of knowledge.

Come on then, sit down and listen, I am about to give it both barrels. But before I do…

THE SECOND DISCLAIMER AND I PROMISE THIS IS THE LAST ONE

Look, I'll be honest, I started writing this book in the Summer of 2019 and it was to coincide with my Edinburgh Fringe show of the same name. My show 'Buddhism And Other Such Rubbish' was a mishmash of my thoughts on the very subjects in this book, but like all stand-up comedians I was trying to make it funny as well. A comic needs a laugh every 15 seconds or he/she is toast. I'm not talking by the way about the comedians who just deliver Ted talks these days and call it stand-up; they're not in my gang — you'll have to speak to them about their separate art form. I've my pride and to do a show with no laughs is personally against my comedy religion.

So, what I'm trying to say is the book was shaping up but wasn't ready in time to shamelessly sell from a trestle table after the daily performances in August stacked in a place where the audience are walking past to leave the building, hopefully in raptures about the show. I wanted to then get it done for the autumn, but my work schedule was so heavy there was no way I'd finish it in 2019. I began working on more of it in 2020 and it looked like it could have had a Spring release and then of course we all know what happened in March 2020!

Yes, I'm aware this does sound like a boy explaining why his homework hasn't been handed in, but it's so much more than that. The whole ethos of the book is now accentuated as a result of this pandemic. The people talking at great length about who caused it, what caused it, what we could've done to prevent it, how there'll be a second spike, whether methods to combat it are the right methods, even calls that the virus doesn't even exist are now surely at the forefront of a book that's about me trying to give practical examples of how people make shit up as they go along and proclaim themselves experts.

So I thought as a sort of tribute to the now naïve looking world we once lived in and the worldly wise almost post-apocalyptic one we live in now but with nothing blown up and nothing flattened save for a few statues, I've kept all the old material in as well as all the new post-Covid stuff that bombards you daily on news sites and social media platforms.

Also, as a result of living in the UK and the Chancellor not giving any grants to people who are self-employed and running a limited company, I now work! I'm a part time delivery man, dropping parcels of alcohol, snacks and household items on people's doorsteps late at night. I earn enough to get by and hopefully it'll keep me going till the gigs all start up after the virus is under control. Who knows when that will be, if ever.

So the thing I wrote previously about me always being a comedian has taken an unexpected twist. There you go, you don't know what's round the corner, do you. I'd like to think though that the sentiment in this book isn't any different and we go again!

Anyway as you were and er hum take two...

LET'S ALL GET ON THE SAME PAGE

Right, I hope you enjoy this book. This book is all about me exploring the way that British people in these times and in times of the recent past behave in the medium of knowledge. It's people's knowledge, or lack of knowledge, that I'm trying to explore and present to you in this book. It's the way people either blag their way through subjects or whether they genuinely think that they're a fountain of knowledge on said subject. The reason I'm making this clear at the beginning is because it's not about bullshitters or liars, this is a different phenomenon altogether, although it's practised often by the same people.

We've all met bullshitters, we've gone to school with lying bastards and then when we think we are shot of them because we've walked out of school for the last time, the most extraordinary thing happens but it's not extraordinary when we look back... we end up working with them.

Now this bit is specifically aimed at a specific type of bullshitter and that's the fantasist, the one that can pull these ridiculous anecdotes out of the air where they themselves are almost always the hero of the completely made-up tale. The fantasists themselves very often don't even realise that they're a figure of fun when they're not there, that they make people's faces light up when someone regales a party of people with another one of his made-up antics when he's not about. 'Tell him about Rodney', 'has he heard the one about when he supposedly apprehended that mugger outside of Heworth Metro station and got the medal for bravery?', then there's a shared delight and crackle of glee that someone hasn't heard this outlandishly nonsensical story, so someone tells the tale and everyone else doesn't mind hearing it again like it was a drinker's fairy tale that never gets old.

Stand-up comedy and the British stand-up comedy circuit for which I have been trooping the boards since the mid 1990s has, as you can imagine, produced its most ludicrous of fantasists, it's created probably no more or no less than other industries that I've worked in, but of course the lies are more grandiose and of course in an industry where you already get the chance to work with legendary film directors, famous actors, politicians, sports stars, people in the pop world and so on, the stories have to be even more mind blowing than the usual bloke down the pub bullshit that people indulge in to impress a long in the tooth stage performer who has seen it all in terms of audacity and theatrical derring-do coupled with stinging put-down lines. If there's a bunch of hard drinking 20 years plus in the game comedians round a table, the story has to hit a high watermark.

No, it's not about that lot, but as I say these people do tend to indulge in knowledge fraud to an epidemical level so they may get a nod between now and the end of the book.

The people that I'm levelling this whole long diatribe at are the ones who think they can read Wikipedia about something huge like Buddhism and feel they can then argue with a devout Buddhist and come out victorious, the ones that spend a fortnight in the Algarve and try and tell you all about Portuguese culture, the ones who knew an intellectual who was a bit scatter-brained so therefore they all are, the ones who can cast off a whole industry in nine words 'bunch of bolshy bastards the whole lot of them'.

Now before we get into this, I'll say it now: I'm guilty of both the things I've touched on. I've embellished stories to make them more interesting, I've set the scene rather like a film and given the story dramatic pauses and created a mundanity that gets blasted out of the water so as to accentuate the outrageous part and to make for the light and shade of the tale. I do this sort of thing for a living, so I know how it works.

I'd say I've got 5% bullshitness in me, but no more; when I was younger it was more like 15-20, maybe even more than that, but now it's down to a safe 5% now that I'm 50 years old. I reckon if you've no bullshit at all in you, then you're probably mentally ill or a devout Christian or you're a mass murderer, or all three. Someone who doesn't lie at all should be avoided and that perversely is the most honest thing I'll say in this whole book. I reckon the average bullshit merchant has about 75-80% bullshit in them. I'd say most people are in a 2-15% level of bullshitness which is safe, it's like a normal blood pressure. There's not many between 15 and 75 – why would there be?!! I don't know anyone who's a fantasist some of the time but then decides to be straight as a dye on other occasions; you're either a silly old liar or you're not. They stick out like people with a rare blood group or being left-handed. You're either a fantasist or you're a well-adjusted person who doesn't really need to lie on an industrial level, especially not indulging in lies that you think might make you a more interesting jet set type of person. Are we born like that or is it nurtured, or is it a reaction to be being shunned and neglected? Not my concern and not what this book is about, it's the way it is, and if you want to get into the psychology or certainly the sociology of it, then pick up a different book

My family weren't liars as such, at least as far as I'm aware they weren't. My mother was probably highest out of our household, she must have got to the 10% level over her lifetime, she did that housewife thing of using phrases like 'and he waltzed into the place thinking everyone would recognise him' when someone simply walked into a room, you know the type of thing, 'they wanted the ground to come and swallow them up all the great clichés. I think a lot of it was just adding dramatic effect to a tale or a bit of gossip that I've covered already. My father didn't indulge in made-up stories at all to the best of my knowledge, and my sister was an honest person who didn't feel the need to invent scenarios or situations where she came out on top time and again to prove how great and iconic she was. Sadly, all three are dead now and while I miss them all very much, I'm glad they had lives that they didn't need to enhance through the medium of bullshit.

As far as my current family goes, my partner is very honest, almost too honest, so much so that she can't even bring herself to be economical with the truth for the greater good or downplay how bad something is to soften blows; our daughter is very straight and hasn't been brought up in a braggart's type of household so as far as I'm aware she's no fantasist. So there you go, my flesh and blood is fairly clean.

I'm not saying this in a smug way, as it's alright to be a bit of a liar in my opinion, you're still okay to live your life — it can land you into trouble with the law if you do it at the wrong time, but in the main, if you are that way inclined and know it in your heart of hearts (because I'm convinced all bullshitters do), bullshit away because you are part of the rich fabric of life, but do expect ridicule and scorn and in some instances downright hatred from others — not from me I must stress, but there are others in life who will not take to your lies at all. You have been warned.

As I say though, this book isn't about the liars, the enhancers and chancers, the perjurers, embellishers and spinners of yarns – those people can be summed up very quickly and the bottom line is, whatever the subject, they've got a story to top it off. People are aware of this lot, 'If you've been to Tenerife, he's been to Elevenerife' yes we're all close to one of those, they live on every street. They're not the subject of a book in my opinion; no, it's more the deluded, the ones who need to go out more, study more, work that knowledge muscle more, but who think that their existing knowledge is tip top and that no one will get the better of their understanding of the subject in hand. It's with that I'll make a start.

THESE ARE MY OPINIONS

Let's get this straight before we get into it: I have opinions. They're forthright and they're entertaining in my opinion. See, there's another opinion right there. The opinions I have might not be exactly the same as your opinions, but they're mine and that should be celebrated not scrutinised or belittled just as yours should. They change, yes they've changed down the years, in fact they've changed on a daily basis but then they've invariably landed back to my original thoughts that I had on the said subject. I've gone with my gut feeling and I've been right; well I'll rephrase that, I feel that I have been right. Sometimes I change my opinion to myself and give myself caveats to stimulate debate with myself, it's my opinions but in true 'numbskulls' style they're bashed out by a vocal committee residing in my head. If you're not comfortable at this point and that you feel that you're reading the book of a schizophrenic psychopath, then by all means bail out now because it's not going to change. I say what I say but I thrash it about with the friends living in my head. I try and think about what I say, but like everyone I've been prone to opening my mouth and letting anger, abuse, passion, sentiment, pettiness, divisiveness but also diplomacy, self aggrandisement and silliness come out as well as a lot of other things rather than saying something good. Don't take with a pinch of salt what I say because I would say it all holds water, but at the same time don't think it's the thoughts of someone with a great mind of our time. As I say, these are my opinions and I'm sure you have yours. Same as the fact that everyone has a life story and everyone's is discernibly different. Your opinion can be different to mine and just as compelling, but this is what I think.

They're not my principles though, principles tend to mean you want to live by your opinions or you have to judge others by them. I don't really have consistent principles, I think that's a very silly way to be because things can change in society and your principle all of a sudden looks very 'Cholmondley Warner' in a modern world. I've not been around forever, but in my half century I've seen so many attitudes change so I'll have a few non acted on principles but they'll change; however, others won't notice because I wasn't flaunting my original principles about the place like a rogue with stolen Gillette razors in a Gateshead High Street pub in the first place. So many people like to flag up that they 'said this was going to happen yeeeeeeeaaaaaars ago' about something that's turned out the way that they thought it would but don't realise how they've conveniently forgotten stuff they predicted that didn't happen at all. It's like how a gambler talks about his big wins but neglects to mention the routine failures and the ritual of being rinsed on a daily basis by the bookmaker who makes a living out of bet hedging.

Here's a quick one to be going on with and it comes from a so-called political heavyweight from the past who at the time of writing is still alive and at the ripe old age of 96. Kenneth Kaunda, the long-time president of Zambia, was a guest on ITV's TVAM's weekend show in 1987 and was talking to presenter David Frost about unrest in South Africa after yet more trouble in the streets of Johannesburg on that particular week. I remember watching this and not believing what I was hearing. Frost was at pains to remind Kaunda and the viewers of his 'visionary genius' by saying "Of course, Kenneth, you predicted all this years ago, didn't you" and he went on to explain that in the 60s and 70s Kaunda was telling Frost and others that if there wasn't reforms from the white minority government, there would be, get this, civil unrest and in many cases riots. Well I bloody never, eh! I remember as a lad asking my dad what would happen in South Africa if the apartheid regime carried on much longer, and do you know what? He said the same. His words were that the whole thing would blow up. I'm sure many others of the same generation thought the same too, only they weren't political leaders paid for a considered opinion, just plain Joe Smiths of this world who read newspapers. Apart from the fact that he stated the bleeding obvious, Kaunda hardly stuck his neck out did he, to say that there might be a few more ructions when there was civil disorder in the first place; and do you know what the nice irony was? He was sort of wrong! Three years later Nelson Mandela was released from prison by President

FW de Klerk and both sides met in the middle so to speak, and a compromise was reached culminating in a free and fair election a few years after where of course Mandela's ANC party swept to power with a landslide majority. No real bloodshed, just a realisation that the old ways couldn't carry on. Kaunda wasn't a visionary, he had just backed the 20 to 1 on a horse at the delayed race but wanted it each way.

By the way, due to this book being written over two years, Kaunda is indeed dead now, yes I can't put him right about an interview I'm sure he forgot about not long after!

Remember the great quote of Groucho Marx: 'Those are my principles and if you don't like them... well, I have others.' That to me sums it all up. I like stepping up to the plate and telling people what I think, I like it even more when it's in the face of bullies like we see on social media these days. Some people don't like other people's opinions, they get very tetchy when others haven't somehow worked it out like they have, and it shows. My favourite is when people say something online and put FACT at the end of it in uppercase letters – you've seen it before, haven't you. 'There was no minimum wage before Tony Blair FACT', 'We've won the league six times and that's the biggest title you can win FACT', 'You can say all you like, The Ramones were the first punk band FACT' – it's as if saying fact but saying it in capitals is the real defining moment of the debate, the heavyweight boxer's big shots that make their opponents go down on the canvas in their own heads of course. The 'FACT' platoon have never lost a debate though, have they, they breeze through life thinking 'that told the bastards, that shut them up, those people with the wrong opinions that shouldn't be allowed to have them because they're wrong' – you know the types relaying stories where the person that they were arguing with was apparently always struggling against their irresistible force and ,metaphorically gasping, hanging on to the ropes when they swept in and gave the final fatal blow, you know the moments 'So I said to him and so who's going to pay for all of that what you're proposing? And he said well I, well I, well I think and I said well nothing!'.

Also let's hear it for the opinionated. I think it's become a derogatory phrase in recent years, probably because of the actions of the very people I'm attacking in this book; that is, the people with opinions but without any knowledge or experience to back those vacuous opinions up. I have, however, got no problem with the people who offer out an opinion, be it in depth or just a soundbite when they do already know stuff. It's their business if they decide to tell you about the subjects they know all about in great detail, if they want to appear like an idiot savant character and give you fuck all then that's up to them as well. Two great and diverse examples of recent history being Brian Clough and Margaret Thatcher, two people I don't have much time for myself unlike great swathes of this nation. I will give them a nod though and acknowledge their smartness for the fact that they sort of 'moron-ed' it up for the camera so a whole load of plain speaking, tell it like it is types who revelled in liking the simple things in life and being straightforward and ordinary thought these people were great and hung on their every word. 'Oh I like him, he says what he thinks' — fuck me what dangerous ground that is!! 'Thatcher was the best PM in peace time history, she put the great back into Britain because what needed to be done got done by her, there was no messing around' — oh no, we're in trouble if someone thinks not thinking things through is a virtue!

Yes, those people brought the worst out of many a person and I think it's proved that they did some pretty bad things, but this country in my opinion has been enhanced and entertained by their very existence. I feel that their supposed radical approach has made them very similar and they're from the same generation with the same working class Presbyterian values (I know Thatcher was Methodist and maybe Clough's family were, but you get the idea), but ironically I know that Clough hated the woman and was a big Labour man. Whenever either of them were interviewed though, in my view you never got the real them, you just got a ridiculous caricature which got more ridiculous the older and more fucked up and faded away they got. They believed their own press and they both went on too long. There you go, I hope that's pissed a few people off reading this, cue silly voice 'ah yeah and what have you achieved in your life, mate'?

Anyway let the opinions commence, feel free to get angry, tell me to fuck off while looking at the words on the page, shake your head (I like that one) and quote bits to whoever's in the room with you, prefacing it with this line "have you heard this bit?"!

I DON'T KNOW STUFF

I honestly wish I knew things, practical things, but also master-class levels of things. I wish I had an organic natural aptitude for stuff, I wish I could just take a quick look at something and say to myself 'yes I've seen this sort of thing before' and practically apply everything I've learned to solving the problem I face. I wish I had an eye for a design, had a way of spotting talent, waves of inspiration to make life easier or to save myself some money, I wish I could foresee worldwide events changing and use it to my benefit. I wish I could use an extensive knowledge of practical philosophy to make my own observations on life, the universe and everything.

Wishing is one thing, having an honest appraisal of your lack of knowledge is quite another. I'm very proud of my brutal honesty, my non-self-aggrandisement and my perverse pride of knowing very little about fucking anything.

Why should I know stuff? Why not would be the contradictory argument. Well I would say that you have to know stuff about things you're interested in, surely? I mean then what's the point in taking an interest, you have to at least have a passing knowledge, don't you? Yes, I'll give you that, you get into a subject it would be hatstand to then punish yourself by not having any knowledge on it. However, when it comes to other things, oh I don't know, the welfare system in America, the works of Dickens, mean temperatures in different global areas on the tundra line, the rise of distemper, Cat Stevens albums, I could go on, it's a case of why should I be interested? If I wanted to formulate an argument, I might look at a couple of facts about these aforementioned things, you know a couple of memorable bullet points, but I wouldn't study these subjects at my leisure if I wasn't bothered about them.

Do you know about stuff? Would you call yourself an expert in a few subjects? Do you 'know a thing or two' on this or that? If the answer is yes, then maybe you shouldn't be reading this book. You either do have an extensive knowledge of lots of subjects and therefore why would you waste a day or two listening to the ramblings of a stand-up comedy journeyman, or you don't but think you do and throughout this book you'll gradually dislike the author. I can live with that.

Michael Gove was once cut off in mid-sentence on a Sky News show and is now responsible for one of the mighty infamous Tory quotes of his own era, rather like Norman Tebbit (also slightly misquoted) for the phrase 'Get out on your bike and find a job' back in the early 80s. In my view he deserved it though, but hey that's just my own opinion!

Back to Gove though and he was being interviewed on Sky News by Faisal Islam who put it to him that there were a number of economists and organizations of economic prestige that questioned the arguments for leaving the EU and said that it would be a mistake if we did. Gove countered it by saying people have had enough of experts from organizations with acronyms that have got things so wrong in the past. And Faisal Islam, as a skilled interrogator and doing what any populist, seeing politics as a bit of a ratings game for the Mark Corrigan from Peep Show types in this country, cut him off halfway, so while he completed his sentence he took the first half and said 'people have had enough of experts, Michael'!??

Now I'm not here to defend, in my opinion a scummy shyster like Michael Gove, but on this occasion he was done up like a kipper by journalist. This was about a seismic political event of our times, but I'd say it applies all across the board and sums up what this book is about. I think the very folk Gove was getting at was these people that give themselves fancy titles, wear suits, have posh but sort of Thames estuary posh accents, use the industry/trade speak of the day, pull out random statistics that could prove anything, call the other people out of touch or better still racist, and then collect their money and their accolades and continue to be wheeled out on telly or radio as an 'expert'. The very fact is some of these experts get things spectacularly wrong time and again and yet they still get consulted for their 'expertise'.

I once met a bloke who was head of a campaign to help get a new TV channel started in the North of England and it was his job to try and speak to the right people then put a bid in to get a franchise. I met him only briefly for a sort of meeting-cum-get-together with potential contributors to the channel and I couldn't put my finger on it, but his casual arrogance tempered with laid back slap-dashness and a non-commitment to introducing himself to people properly or even sit in a chair properly said to me that we had the wrong great white hope boxing for us. Someone told me though that he knew him well from the past and had a lot of experience, he told me he was part of the stop tuition fees campaign or whatever it was called and more recently the campaign to have an independent North East parliament. Ah great! Someone involved in two popular campaigns that managed to, against all the odds, concoct a way of fucking losing heavily. I mean how anyone could be proud of the latter, I don't know! A campaign that had lots of support from lots of people in the region in which I live as a good idea and how exciting it would be to look after our own affairs, to a landslide defeat on the night of the referendum amidst cheering from a baying crowd and a bunch of white, fat, out of touch businessmen cheering and (rightly so because they'd pulled off the impossible) taking the accolades in a crowded town hall, the rest of the country watching on and thinking that regional assembly was now dead in the water for other parts of the country because the yes campaign was so weak as piss. Yes, this bloke was leading us and the next thing I heard was there was a change of tack and the regional channel never happened and didn't get funding. I genuinely can't remember the bloke's name but typically he had a suit, he was quite posh, a sort of neutral accent and no doubt after this pasting he would be headhunted to front up some other anaemic manifesto that magically turns the popular into the unpopular.

There's so many examples of the suits that know nowt but there's plenty with the overalls and the lab coats that don't know stuff as well. It's just a case of how well you carry it off.

Here's a great example: photography. I've met many a person who says stuff to the tune of 'I'm going to pursue the photography full time I think, I've been asked to do a few jobs and I'm thinking of sending some flyers and business cards out in the area'. Do you know people who suddenly decide that they're now photographers? I bet you do!! They tend to go on undeterred, 'I did the photos for my Auntie and Uncle's golden wedding anniversary, they said I did a great job they were really pleased with the pics'...of course they were, no decent family are going to say 'eeeeh our Derek, these are shit', then they carry on, 'I'm going to lend a friend's studio and I've bought a brand new Canon 70D' yes can I just stop you there, you're not a photographer, what you've done is... you've bought a camera!!

What the Walter Mittys don't realise is that there are camera clubs all over the country and indeed in every free Western country, people get a grounding for it there, some show great aptitude whereas others just enjoy the experience. Having a camera can probably provide you with hours of fun — I'm not knocking that nor am I having a go at people who actually get quite good at taking pictures — but being artistic and finding a mood for a photo and taking an iconic shot is quite another level of talent.

While there may be someone who slips the net and shows a great natural aptitude for taking sublime shots, most people that snap away are no different from you or I, yet the only difference being that they maxed out their credit card to pretend that they had a special eye for moments captured in time, yet we were mere muggles that couldn't reach their level in a million years. Do you get the idea of the people I'm getting at now?!!

There's a lovely Royal example. Prince Edward, or Prince Edward Earl of Wessex as he is now, was the head of a media 'empire' for a while. After failing to make the grade as a Royal Marine officer (his Mam and Dad had to bail him out), he decided he would start his own production company called Ardent where he would make television programmes — I know, the amount of times I've also heard about people in sink council estates make similar types of career decisions is staggering, isn't it. Getting back to the story, he'd done a bit of acting in a couple of theatre companies for about six years with less than glowing reviews from his peers and he had presided over a dreadful show on TV called 'Royal It's

A Knockout' where senior members of the Royal family and popular thespians with ex sports stars and other celebrities joined in this awful PR type charade. I've seen clips and even as an anti-royalist I'm embarrassed for them. He actually took the huff at the end of the programme where he said to press photographers and journalists "I hope you enjoyed it"; after a nervous silence he said, "well what did you think of it?!!", the immediate retort was a simultaneous guffaw from the gathered tribe of hacks, and his answer to that was "thanks" and he turned tail and left the room.

Anyway, he had this company called Ardent and he insisted that they wouldn't be making royal programmes even though that was his one distinct advantage over all his competitors, but that of course was what he ended up doing after a few years because the work was drying up. After Alan Partridge type programmes were made like 'Real Tennis', a political soap opera canned after 10 episodes (I'm not making this stuff up!) and a Holocaust drama as well as a show about Sex And The Disabled called Forbidden Pleasures, they were struggling and reduced to making stuff for regional telly where the budget is miniscule. Their saving grace was in America where they have as one knows a healthy obsession with the House of Windsor. A programme called Royalty From A to Z was made and with it a disastrous attempt to invade the privacy of his nephew Prince William by filming him as he was studying at St Andrew's University. This lid-lifting programme was too late though to save the company and its chronic lack of commissions, and he severed all ties with his venture in the early noughties after losses year upon year. I don't know the bloke personally and I'm not intending this book to turn into an eat the rich exercise, but it's clear that it's another case in this country of 'well a load of plebs can do this, there's nothing to stop me then' which is rife in our society, especially with the ultra rich social club pretending that they're getting by in the rat race.

And here to close this section is a quote from Edward himself talking about the British media. On a business trip to the United States on behalf of his television production company, Ardent Productions, he said "they hate anyone who succeeds".

Where do you start? The amount of people with extensive knowledge in all things broadcasting but things like race, background and lack of beneficial contacts holding them back is there for all to see. You don't have to look hard to find folk that should have been given far bigger and better projects in television and film behind the camera than they ever did, but it never happened; and do you know what, that's life, it's never perfect. When it came to the Earl of Wessex though, for some reason his lack of knowledge, know-how and talent that he's blissfully unaware of isn't what made him make risible television programmes, it was the fact that those evil people in British journalism hate successful people like him even though it sort of appears that he... erm... er, hasn't been very successful.

That lack of self-awareness is something I dearly hope I haven't got — please tell me if I'm deluded, it would be kinder in the long run. Maybe I got a better grounding in life at Blaydon Comprehensive School than he ever got at Gordonstoun. I'll never be as rich as him but I don't think I'll ever blame my lack of success on the British media for... not liking success?! A lovely oxymoron that must have gone above his head. Perhaps private education is a load of old bollocks, after all?? Sorry I've just indulged in a short phrase that this very book is having a go at!!

I DO KNOW STUFF

I was doing myself down earlier, not in that self-effacing way that people think will make them more charming in polite society, nor in the clunky working class 'love me love me I'm thick' way either. I thought I'd tell you from the get-go about how little I know about specific subjects, but here's the thing, I do know about stuff as well. It's not stuff you can put a label on or stuff that requires you to pass an exam, but in my time on this planet from an inauspicious start (living in a crap County Durham town which sort of got wiped out when the new Metropolitan borough council bagged it up in 1974 is definitely an inauspicious start, believe me), I've managed slowly but surely to learn how to live and learn how to cope, how to deal with people and how to, in a sense, get on. We all do, but we all do it in unique ways due to us all being on an individual journey. It sounds like a cliché, but all my lessons are life lessons and to sound another cliché klaxon I've spent a long time at the university of life. What have I learned? Well, I tell you what I've learned. I've learned to be able to talk to people. Some might scoff at this, but I've met so many people who can't communicate with folk outside of their own family or of their own ilk. This happens at every level or sub level of class in this country, that of course is because there's no commitment in this country to bring people together, it's my view that governments, be they Conservative or NEW Labour (they're the only parties I can ever see running this island) are only interested in keeping communities apart and encourage them to have disparate worlds of thought. I can, probably due to my job as a stand-up comedian, connect with all walks. I can talk to a middle class crowd, a real bunch of pretentious middle class people can take to me but I can never make it look like I've pandered to them. It's a sort of confidence trick that you learn doing my ridiculous job for a long time, they can see me as a cheeky chappie or a working class philosopher, or some quirky bloke from the poor house who 'doesn't realise how good he is', I've had that patronising one thrown at me several times. I can talk to upper middle class people as well, I can play the house idiot or the house working class person if I want, but I choose not to, good people in my business can, they can instantly find an area where they can click and home in on that. I can talk to my own people whoever they are but I can find them, I can't really put into words who they are but they're about; I can talk to the hard-nosed working classes partly because I'm able to find the common ground due to my job, but mainly because I went to a rough comprehensive school in the Gateshead borough during the early to mid 80s and I worked on building sites and in factories for six years. I stood on the Gallowgate end at St James's Park for about 15 years and played Sunday morning football. I can drop a gear and keep people on board, and I can step it up a bit and bring the pseudo intellectuals with me. Seven-eight thousand comedy gigs has taught me all that and more.

A good mate of mine who is a veteran stand-up comedian and has been in a couple of cult British films, Jeff Innocent, is from London gangster stock. It goes back several generations. He didn't get into the underworld himself, but he was aware who everyone was and was brought up amongst them. He's a fiercely intelligent and sharp bloke as well, very well read and a real scholar when it comes to British social history, with a degree in that field to boot. He's a communist and a supporter of unions and workers. He's also (as you can imagine being a great comedian) got a sense of irony and a sense of sardonic realism about all his ideals and other people's as well. He's a rounded individual and has passed on some great thoughts to me. I'll never forget what he said once and that was "When you live in a predominantly working class or underclass area, your first contact with the outside world on an average day is invariably confrontation". That is so correct. I've found myself throughout my adult life going into a newsagent in the morning and either asking someone to stop being so aggressive, or more often than not minding my own business as someone loses their shit with the shop owner over nothing. Sometimes you have to deal with people shoplifting either by calling them out on it or turning a blind eye (I've always turned a blind eye). Racism is rife and often a boomer type is making editorial comments usually from an aggressive right wing rallying cry perspective when talking to the shop owner about something on the front of the paper. Either that or there's a nasty vibe in the air when people go into the Asian-owned shops and there is mistrust and hostility from both sides. To negotiate these situations and to let some stuff go, as well as not sticking out like a sore thumb as posh middle-class people would, is something that's taken me years to learn properly. If you think this is all bollocks, then by all means say, but I'm fairly sure I know what I mean and I hope others reading this do too. The other confrontation elements certainly in my local area are when you're driving along and people are just crossing the road on a pedestrian crossing even though it's a green light, it's clearly red on the crossing. I tend not to beep my horn or shout out of the window because I know what I'll get, a big hearty 'fuck off cunt' or 'come on then son I'll fuckin fight you'. There would be no 'discussion' about it.

One time I was giving a lift to a posh white feller (I think he was another stand-up comedian) and dropping him off in North London before I negotiated the M1 for the six-hour drive back home to Newcastle (yes, it's no picnic, this stand-up lark!). We were driving along in the Camden-cum-North Euston area when two black blokes just casually walked across the road. This was late at night and they definitely were inviting us to slam on the brakes and have a go at them. They both sauntered across the road staring me out as they dared me to run them over. I just drove slowly around them and then got my speed up and carried on.

"Wow, they were really out of order, why didn't you stop and have it out with them?" the young posh comedian said. "I certainly would have," he added with some confidence in his plummy tone.

"I didn't stop because I value my life and it really wasn't something worth getting wound up about," I calmly replied.

I did mention they were black because it throws into doubt my intentions and probably exposes a slither of prejudice in me which I'm happy to expose — I'm all about honesty and it's just my age at the time and background and stuff you read. However, it also brings forth how I have a degree of realism and it comes through experience. These blokes were trouble, and that, in my wealth of experience of rough lonely cities late at night, I could see that this was not going to end well if I'd got out of the car and confronted them. All you can imagine is that my epitaph would be some dreadful Daily Mail front page about how two nice men were murdered for apparently nothing with a semi racist editorial and some anger on the BBC news bulletin with tension on the streets and a bit of heavy handed policing in that area for a few days, that and both me and the other bloke's respective grieving families being approached by Britain First to join their organisation. There would be an interview with a hard line 'hang em, flog 'em' MP and another one who thought that it was all to do with not enough funding for youth clubs for BAME communities in North London. After a few days it would pass, and people would be back talking about Strictly and The Premier League.

I've learned to walk away at the right time and learned to not even have a political opinion or an opinion about what's right and what's wrong in moments like that, but just to walk away. Maybe if I'd seen this situation through to its self-righteous end, there perhaps would have been a frank exchange of views and then they may have nobly backed down and said 'sorry, bruv, you mind how you go' but I very much doubt it, and you can call me a racist as much as you like, I genuinely don't care because I'm here to tell the tale. The posh bloke though was happy to walk straight to his own death or at least his own thorough kicking, which makes you wonder about have-a-go heroes, doesn't it.

I've spoken to others as well about pubs and how you can gauge how rough they are. A working class person, or should I say a 'comprehensive school' person, can spot trouble in a pub a mile off. You have to trust me on this. It's a sort of radar, maybe it could be called 'mur-dar' I don't know. I've been in pubs with posh people and I've said, 'I think we should leave', and they've innocently asked why and I've pointed out to them the numerous reasons, mainly people looking at us the wrong way, but it's easy to spot the other symptoms. The banter at the bar, the veiled threats that I've heard so many times and a lot of this goes back to the mid-1980s, the very nadir of polite behaviour in licensed premises, particularly in city centres, as well as what the people look like. I remember pubs in Newcastle city centre in those days, it was very much pre the acid house scene, which was a huge game changer in this country, no one was 'loved up' or tripping, there was no groups of lads with centre partings drinking pints of orange juice or people fist bumping or hugging, this was a few years before all that. It was hard arsed blokes, lots of uncouth women, un-licensed bouncers and you could almost smell the trouble. It always seemed to come from nowhere and it was almost always because someone was staring too long at someone else. The headbutt was a common street move and there was a horrific ritual of seeing a fight in the corner of a pub and thinking it was perfectly legitimate to throw full pint glasses at the general direction of the fracas. I never saw anyone thrown out for this impromptu shotput type behaviour and when the vicious fight stopped, paradoxically I never once saw anyone come over and say 'did one of you lot throw a pint at the area I was fighting in?', it all just seemed to be fair game and fights, and indeed full pints of lager being thrown at the fights were just a hazard of the night. These fights took place in the pubs, in the streets outside of the pubs, in the bus stop, in the taxi queues and the best one was on the bus home; this was known as the 'last bus'. There was nowhere to go on this one whether you were a participant in the fight or one of the unsuspecting spectators. I saw and was nearly involved in some horrible last bus violence, and I'd never like to be involved in it again for as long as I live. The last bus disappeared almost overnight the moment Margaret Thatcher passed legislation in 1988 to open the pubs all day, meaning that they didn't close at 3pm anymore and open again at 6, but more importantly they didn't close at 10.30 and allow people a derisory 10 minutes drinking up time, they now closed at 11pm and you had an amazing 20 minutes of relative luxury to see your drinks off. This was a masterstroke whether they'd intended it or not, because some people so set in their ways left at 10.40 and got on the bus even though the buses were now running later services (understandably) and this was not the last bus anymore; others left when time was called just before 11 and got themselves a bus that left just after the hour; and others taking their time to see their drinks off tended to get the very last bus at any time depending upon where you lived between 11.30 and 11.45. Others headed for nightclubs and bars that had licences for a later hour if they sold food. Some would get taxis as they suddenly became much more affordable in these times. In the case of Newcastle, if people were coming from Northumberland or County Durham it was more economically viable for four to share a taxi.

Anyway, I'm getting off the point! The last bus as a result of these Catherine wheel type events was now a goner and anyone under 50 would struggle to remember the hedonism and almost nihilistic chaos of a 'last bus home'. It's consigned to the dustbin of history, which is good, but I learned a lot from it. I play crowds that are apparently rowdy and unplayable according to other people on the bill; I've no interest in doing well in front of said crowds but whatever happens they're not the last bus to Blaydon from Newcastle in the 80s.

The Viz comic, which not only was a bit of a cult sensation

in this country in the late 80s and early 90s, but seemed to be a bit of a barometer of the crass street scene in Britain particularly post-industrial Northern England at that time. They had I kid you not T shirts for sale in the merchandise section of the mag with 'Did You Spill My Pint' on them. This was actually one of the most common lines trotted out by a perpetrator of violence prior to the first punch or indeed nut to the nose in the city at the time. It was a moronic period of modern social history, but as I say, I can face anything after that grounding.

So in summary, it's not being streetwise as such, but it's being able to talk to the dozen or so levels of class from the very bottom up and indeed sub groups of those levels that I've learned to be adept at just through accident of birth, be that the year and the geography.

HOW MUCH DO YOU REALLY KNOW?

'I AM THE WISEST MAN ALIVE, FOR I KNOW ONE THING, AND THAT IS THAT I KNOW NOTHING' PLATO

Of course Plato (or Socrates who apparently was Plato, are they fucking with us to put us off philosophy?!) was always banging on about how we don't know whether we are truly happier than a mouse or more fulfilled than an ant and stuff like that, and I think Socrates/Plato killed himself in the end so looking at it from 21st century eyes he may well have got some form of personal independence payment and not been hassled to look for work if he had lived today, and I don't know, some regular happy pills, anything for a GP signing somebody off with bad handwriting so he can go and play golf in the afternoon. The truth is though, that you could say to anyone that chucks advice to you 'and what the fuck do you know'? and there'd be something in that in my view. Some people would have seen firsthand Archduke Franz Ferdinand

and his wife being shot in Sarajevo or might have been a train guard when Franco met Hitler on that railway carriage that time, it doesn't mean that they're some sort of sage or that they're more qualified than others to talk about a famous moment in history just because they were close to it.

In my own humble opinion, the best people like the iconic Plato don't profess to know bloody everything. During the Covid-19 daily briefings the scientists would never be drawn on whether there was a vaccine on the way, whether herd immunity was an effective way of bringing the numbers down, or whether it definitely lived better indoors rather than out. The politicians seemed to learn daily that spouting shite about things you knew very little about wasn't really a good look and began taking on the traits of the scientists. The experts looked classier by saying things like 'it would be impossible to surmise at this stage' or 'it would appear with the data that we have that would appear to be the case but it would be presumptuous to say that this is the absolute pattern', you know stuff like that which in my view makes people rest easier than a certain politician talking about 'Whack a mole', 'getting the sombrero flat' and 'beating this thing into submission'.

The great Sir Alex Ferguson, the former St Mirren, Aberdeen, Scotland and of course Manchester United manager, always seemed in retrospective interviews to be explaining how he got something all wrong or how his dithering or not trusting his instincts cost him a good signing. It's really refreshing to hear a man who won all sorts of honours as a football manager and he maintained it year on year, as well as proving his doubters wrong and winning stuff with a relatively small club as well as perhaps the biggest football club in the world, talking publicly about his fundamental flaws and with it huge mistakes. I don't think it's a false modesty, I believe that it's an admission that you have to step up to the plate when you have a big career and sometimes your judgement was not always right. There's an old Yorkshire saying 'make a decision to do something even if it's nowt' and that can apply here.

I've also seen tacit admissions by former advisers to governments and heads of unions or special envoys when talking about important political upheavals from the past on TV documentaries. They explain what the problem was and how they were doing their best, but they misjudged someone or went with the wrong person's guidance and all other fallible stuff that humans do, even ones that have risen to the very top of their field. I don't know about you, but I feel very comforted when I see these interviews, anecdotal examples of retrospective human error.

Finally for this section, I will say that I do have a skill set, it is arbitrary and it's not big, but I do know things, not just the vague stuff about reading people and their body language due to doing public speaking, but specific skills. In short, they are in no particular order: an understanding of cantilevers of beams, trusses and other designs to keep bridges up, a smattering in instrumentation, I can read a

Kempes conversation book and can read a micrometer imperial and metric, I know my way round tool slides and could probably pick up robotics and CAD CAM again pretty quickly if I did a refresher course. I can read first angle projection and third angle projection technical drawings and could probably still tell you all the shorthand terms. I can get by in differentiation in Mathematics and could probably build a locomotive, or nowadays it would be something powered by a motor or an engine where, to be fair, I might have to liaise with an electrical engineer to do it or a mechanical engineer for a four stroke engine. I could still put a roof on, I reckon, I could felt it, lat it and then put the whole thing on including the ridge tiles and the pointing. It might take me ages and the pointing would be a bit shit, but I'm sure someone else could do that; I can gas weld, mig weld and arc weld, none too well but again if I had a bit longer than the people who do it working to a time schedule I can do a fairly shabby but passable job. I could pretend to be a football coach and probably get away with it at a reasonable non-league level until someone asked me for my badges, I could design a poster to a low standard and I could definitely direct a film or a TV recording working with the camera crew and editor. I wouldn't be a celebrated director, in fact I'm sure I'd be very uninspiring, but I'd get the fucking job done and it wouldn't be out and out embarrassing. I could gag up a script and write a half hour sitcom that has a beginning, middle and an end. I could form a crap band and we would be able to record original songs — whether they would be any good would be down to others to decide, but they'd have verses, middle eights and codas if need be, and I could pastiche a style quite easily. I could probably tour a hastily put together band, and again, it may not be good but I could pass an episode of Faking It, of that I have no doubt — 'the only people who know are the musicians and they never pay to get in' the great Ian Dury once said. I know trivia about punk mainly but lots of other musical sub-groups of modern popular music, I could do well on Mastermind with a subject like Football in the 70s, Newcastle United 1970-1990 or Scottish World Cup campaigns throughout history. I could get by on some stand-up comedy routines as well and have a basic knowledge of the history of music hall, variety comedy, the folk scene, alternative comedy and the postmodern circuit. I'm sure there's more stuff I might be able to bluff my way through, but that's the list as far as I can remember.

The one constant about that last paragraph is that I'm not an expert in any of those fields, I just have an interest and a basic knowledge; it's a big difference. Ask me what I'm a real expert in as in someone who really knows his stuff and as has been intimated before it would amount to probably nothing! I know about my job but frankly everyone should be an expert in their own job, otherwise you're stealing a living, aren't you?

Also, what I know about my job I'm not going to tell people. The real matrix type stuff about stand-up comedy, the subtle tricks rather like a magician in the magic circle, I'm not going to just blurt out in a paperback book. Some of the stuff is hard to put into words anyway, it's rather like a jazz or a soul musician telling you about the feel or a poet telling you their inspiration. The other thing about my job which has a huge slice of irony about it is that books explaining comedy are the most unfunny dry books. There are these pricks that say things like 'it can't be taught' but I'm afraid it can — how do you explain <insert name of comic that you as a reader think is dreadful>?!! No, stand-up comedy and indeed sketch comedy can be explained, but it's about as turgid as reading Karl Marx, and as I say I have picked loads of stuff up over the years but I'll keep what I have to myself partly through selfishness and partly through not wanting to bore you to death.

The late great Ken Dodd apparently said that he had a couple of sentences on a piece of paper in a safe in his house and the words on it if they were read out would blow stand-up comedy wide open. That's the great thing about legends like Dodd and why I love stand-up comedians — I'm fairly sure he was talking out of his arse and winding people up, but no one really knew and no one seemed to bring it up in the weeks after he'd died. It probably said something like 'be more spontaneous' on a piece of paper or some sort of Doddy-type joke; the fact is people like Ken Dodd were so immersed in their job and lived stand-up that you couldn't begin to see him do something as clunky and binary as a comedy class telling Laura the 30 something Loss Adjuster that she needs to release her inner clown because her stories about how her husband doesn't lift a finger in the house are really original.

He did his thing, never told people of his method, he just told jokes when people in serious interviews asked, and had a long, long career just doing more and more shows. He did say that he was always improving as a comic and obviously when one gig was finished the next thing to think about was the next show. He was the ultimate expert in his craft, but he just saw it as his trade, his thing that he did. Was he a one off? But perhaps others aren't like that? Maybe people in the main aren't experts in their own jobs and maybe that's why we are in debt to the Chinese and that people actually listen to self-appointed political pundits like Owen Jones and Darren Grimes, instead of real experts.

EMPTY VESSELS

The old saying empty vessels make the most noise, of course is not a 100% fact — there are exceptions to these rules — but I have noticed time and time again that the most vacuous people always seem to hammer home their limited knowledge till it gets tiresome. Their reasoning and their techniques to get you to their way of thinking have conical levels of narrowness. There are so many empty vessels in this country, why? I could give you a back of a fag packet explanation if you'd like to hear it? Yes of course there are so many different theories and counter theories and sub theories but here's my pot shot.

In this country we're taught practical things, our schools are like big children factories installing and assembling them with big knowledge over an 11-year period. We're big on the Maths and English, English language that is. We like the Physics and Chemistry and all the low-level practical stuff like changing plugs and tyres as well as subjects like Geography, you know grid references, the average rainfall of Swansea or how Middlesbrough grew very quickly because of iron ore in the

Cleveland Hills, all these things are seen as good knowledge. We learn Shakespeare parrot fashion and our history lessons are all pub quiz type facts, '1066, miss', 'The Magna Carta, sir', 'In August 1492, Columbus sailed the ocean blue'. We like to be able to hang curtains and put ceiling roses up and that's just the women (a deliberate cliché comedy club style joke there, calm down). We're meant to be handy with washing machines and we're to be decent at sport. Oh yes, we've all got to have a grounding in sport, apparently it's imperative. It was always hilarious looking back at PE during schooldays seeing an arty kid, really skinny and quite powder puff on the football pitch, the sport obviously wasn't for him, being bellowed at by the track-suited gym teacher who played football professionally as a young man — "how many times have I told you, Thompson, when the full back's got it take your man down the line and dig a hole, create space for him so it brings other players into play, you've obviously not been listening". Yes, it's clear the future David Hockney has got to be a decent left midfielder to get on in life.

Have you noticed though, nobody gets taught philosophy? Did you know it's compulsory in France? We don't get very much on workers' rights or saving money. I've always maintained if a politician came along and was addressing big crowds saying 'don't ever get credit, credit cards are a way of keeping you down, just save up' to the cheers of the crowd, there would be people out there trying to get the fucker bumped off! It's like he's giving away the big secret and needs to be rubbed out.

Napoleon once said that we were the nation of shopkeepers; I don't think people knew exactly what he meant but I can see the sentiment more and more as I get older. Whatever your opinion was on Brexit (and without being a creep I can see pertinent points on both sides), you have to admit the British can never see themselves wanting to be involved in any scheme where they don't personally get anything out of it. Whether that is the British psyche or whether they've been spoon fed that for 500 years so we just go along with it, I don't know.

I always remember a French bloke from the EU years ago (he might have been Belgian I wasn't taking too much notice) on Question Time — the flagship BBC1 Thursday night argument programme between arrogant politicians, arrogant newspaper columnists and arrogant celebrities — say in broken English that the trouble with the British is that when they put a pound into something they want two pounds back! It was very Allo Allo 'Ven zey put a pount in zey vont two pounds back'. He was howled at but not in a humorous way. It was derision on an industrial scale, he couldn't even get a quarter way through the next sentence, British political pantomime mixed with an air of football hooliganism at its finest. We do that air of menace so well on this island, don't we. He was fucking well right, though. Rightly or wrongly we joined something in the 70s where we thought that we'd all do really well out of, that's how it was sold to us like we were in a shop. Of course it wasn't explained to us that it was to make a few rich people richer and the people doing the stocks and shares would do well out of it as well, but in general everyone else was going to have most of their industry taken away to places with cheaper labour and that in 30 years we'd have to be grateful when small grants to pay for a relief road or some industrial units from the very behemoth itself that took our stuff from us in the first place. The thing that annoys people is that we were all lied to, we got taken into something by stealth over a 40-year period, that's the way I see it. We joined because we wanted more prosperity, not so they could raid our piggy bank.

On the other side of the coin though, we've been brought up in this country to just have stuff and assume we can have stuff cos we've paid for it and we've got the receipt and we're British. Long gone are the Calvinist ideals of working hard and every penny going back into the land, we've had 40 years of Thatcherism where we're seen as customers, as consumers and people that want to get something back. The Sun newspaper was all for that; I used to read it every day, unfortunately, between 1986 and 1991; it was always in the canteen at every factory I worked in, that and The Mirror and occasionally The Daily Star. I got a handle on their drip feed editorial every day. Away from the tits and the awful puns and the destroying of a celebrity's career, it was all about the modern working classes and what they were perceived to be all about, it was about working hard, getting tax breaks and not having to pay for scroungers on the dole or single mothers or anyone else they didn't like; that was the overall sentiment. These newspapers made enemies and Brussels was one of those enemies for years and years. 'Those Eurocrats in Brussels want to standardise your sausage!', it's beyond laughable when you think back.

If we had fewer empty vessels we could've had this Euro debate in a much better way, it's descending into chaos because it's a load of white van types arguing with pseudo intellectuals and all the reasonable people are being drowned out by grandstanding buffoons. It's the empty vessels that have the opinions on absolutely everything and however annoying it is, it makes for compulsive listening!

How to solve this? Fuck knows. For a quick pot shot I'd say better satirists on television would be a start — how about some white working class people satirising the news for a change? Some white working class voices ripping the piss out of authority? Some white working class people with entertaining opinions going for the jugular but balancing that by being self effacing and laughing at the irony of it all, ridiculing those in power while pointing out their own people's ridiculous ideologies and their terrible clichés. Maybe those people don't exist? I'd argue that they do and I've been in the industry for over a quarter of a century now and I've met many a smart white working class person with great things to say politically, much better than anything I've heard from the Radio 4 type pseuds.

Phrases like 'the BBC is hideously white' from Greg Dyke really rankles with the white working classes and posh people don't even realise that it does, and even if they did they wouldn't know why the working classes were so angry about it. While newspapers like the Daily Mail find comments like that 'appalling' and are absolutely 'appalled' by it and can't reiterate enough how 'appalling' that comment was, it's all just staged outrage on their part. They're the same people as the people that make those comments, they're from the same social stratosphere, they have the same interests and I bet their core values are very similar.

The people that should be outraged are the white working classes themselves who are pissed on once again. What they mean by 'the BBC is hideously white' is that the BBC is hideously middle class and always has been, using the word 'white' gets the middle class off the hook once again. By making phrases like 'hideously white' it appeases another set of middle class white people who speak for ethnic minorities and it leads to more black and Asian performers and producers and writers being invited to take on commissioned and non-commissioned roles in the network, but not nearly as many as there should be compared to all the white middle class people, but loads more than the white working class people per head of population. Of course, there are white working class people on the television and radio, but compare that to the amount of white middle class people on the television and radio and you'll see where I'm coming from.

The working class comedians that are on telly are taken to the tranquil waters of observational comedy and gentle panel shows along with chat shows, being a professional celebrity and wearing penguin suits at award shows making comments like 'fancy me, little me, working class me being on a show with Meryl Streep' or 'it was a nice spread backstage tonight at the Royal command performance, I couldn't find the pork pies though' cue laughter from cunts thinking 'ha ha very funny stuff from the great unwashed there'. It's the 'good old honest Tommy' again but in a 21st century guise.

These safe, wholesome, middle class satirists that seem to think that they're fighting the good fight and have the government quaking in their boots don't just do their own political comedy shows, oh no they branch out into the history of British culture as well on the small screen and love being these talking heads casting off a whole era or an entire culture at the behest of the producers and commissioners of the programmes that are being made; however, the overall editorial of the programme, ie the title and the bits with the narrator, always stays the same. They're getting their comments in but obviously have no say in what the ethos of the programme is about. There's no blue sky thinking, caveats or opposing views, it's just a reinforcement of what probably some modern-day Lord Grade has decided happened in post-war British history. The shows tend to have naff titles like...

IT WAS ALRIGHT IN THE 70S

Ah yes, a television show where its prime aim is to 'tell' you what it was like in the old days and how it was all very unacceptable and the audience are on side with the protagonist (for the particular unsavoury 1970s clip), who is watching on a giant TV being 'downright appalled' that they got away with such stuff. It's so one sided as a programme yet bizarrely it doesn't realise that it is! Very often the 'can't believe what they're watching' comedian or broadcaster puts their hand to their mouth and lets out an 'oh my god' or 'did they just call her a bitch there?' just so as to augment the anachronism in front of the television viewer's eyes when in actual fact they're just watching a programme from almost 50 years ago and hey, times change!

The very fact that women weren't taken very seriously, gay people were humorous duckies and ethnic minorities were a bit basic but nice people and up for a laugh when white people casually chucked racist stereotypes at them isn't really much of a surprise to the rest of us, certainly not to those of us that lived through the quirky decade itself; to be honest, the television was probably a much milder depiction than how the above people were treated in real life. However, it seems to be an amazing ground-breaking discovery for these posh people, rather like archaeologist Richard Leakey when he discovered the human bones in Ethiopia that were 190,000 years old, when they see Richard Beckinsale or Wendy Craig say something about rape that is a bit laissez faire compared to today's society where you have to put a word like scumbag or horrific before or after the word rape just to prove that you don't approve of it.

I love it when these people decide to make these arbitrary rules whereby no one was ever allowed to have liked these shows in the first place and that they're literally consigned to the dustbin of history (think statues now). It's not just that these shows don't get shown anymore, but once again people must say 'the appalling It Ain't Half Hot Mum' or 'The Offensive Love Thy Neighbour', so as to link them with these words I think they think it will always exorcise their evil spirits and weaken their humour when the passage of time normally does that anyway. We seem to live in an era where the bad stuff must go and go quickly, and then not only that, it should be taboo and therefore forgotten, and then no one can ever like anything that is taboo and forgotten. It's like we must live in a Middle Ages kind of superstitious world to some of the retro gatekeepers, the past must be airbrushed, some of the bad things quietly disposed of, the other bad things belittled and dismissed to the point that people are almost embarrassed to bring them up. It's a mob mentality

Lawson on this and here it is:

However, the objection to those shows is that the assumptions behind the characterisation and writing date from an era of different attitudes to race and therefore risk causing offence now. In contrast, Cleese and Booth, when they wrote the character of Major Gowen, were clearly not being unthinkingly racist; rather, they were satirising an English upper-class bigot. The joke depends on the audience first thinking that, when the Major rebukes his companion "No, no, no", he is condemning her for inflammatory language, when it turns out that he is simply a particularly pedantic racist. A liberal pedant might object that it was odd of the BBC to cut just that one line from the episode in question as the entire premise of The Germans is English post-second world war humour and hostility towards the country. But, while the show will never win a prize for encouraging Anglo-German cultural understanding, Cleese is comically depicting — rather than politically promoting — fear of "Fritz".

Most viewers of Fawlty Towers, then and now, are sophisticated enough to understand the difference between this and Love Thy Neighbour, which had bigotry as a central theme and arguably an underlying impulse in the writing.

Fast forward to 2020 and as I was driving one night, I heard some race relations woman who had put pressure on UKTV for the censorship on BBC Radio Five Live talking to presenter Tony Livesey. This lady, who was clearly white and to be fair not someone with a rah rah right on accent rather an M62 generic North of England twang, was telling us the reasoning behind the decision to pull the line out from the broadcast of the show. 'We felt that we had to take that line out because although language like that may have been acceptable at that particular time and I'm not having a go at people thinking that it was acceptable to use racial slurs like that at the time, we feel that we've moved on and we don't think audiences today deem words like that acceptable.' To reiterate what Mark Lawson so eloquently put all those years ago, the whole point was you as a viewer were laughing at the backward nature of the Major's observation and you're with Basil Fawlty on this joke when he rolls his eyes at the bigoted nature of this silly old man. It seems, however, to go above this bull's knacker's head that in 1975 we were actually much more forward thinking and woke than perhaps we are now and that this exchange between Basil and the Major reinforces that. Also, it's very funny the whole left turn of it. Amazing though that in race relations we have these sense of humour vacuums who like to ban this and censor that, but obviously have no clue about the history of something like a sitcom where for example 'Till Death Do Us Part' did race relations a power of good because it got (to quote the late Tony Booth) white working class British people to watch the programme and the programme more or less said to them 'have a long hard look at yourselves.' Of course with that particular sitcom you got people saying 'yes but what if some people take Alf Garnett's views seriously then etc etc'. Fine, just get rid of all comedy and have some nice shows where no one is ever mean. Christ, what a scary country that would be.

XENOPHOBIA AND REGIONALISM

Are these tolerable? It's ambiguous but I'm going to let the whole dislike of the foreigners and the other parts of the country stuff pass. I mean for fuck's sake, having a go at a country or a region and making fairly vague but inflammatory remarks about them is hardly a Hitler type of nationalist hysteria or Pol Pot or an African post second world war military dictator wanting the entire north part of his country wiped out just because he doesn't like them. They're words from people of a low intellectual level that aren't worth taking to one's bed over.

Sometimes regionalism can actually be great fun. The comedy circuit in the 90s used to be full of comperes and satirists who did jokes about Glaswegians, Scousers, Geordies, Cockneys and other people from parts of this island that had a strong cultural identity; and although it was step 1 on the stereotype level, it always seemed to be good craic and people laughed at the ridiculousness of it all and it was never taken too seriously. A bit of light relief in what is a fraught old life where, if we're lucky, we only get 70 odd years of and a good third of that is being a pensioner or a kid. So, some smart arse with a microphone said that your town was full of rogues who don't like to work and people around you have thrown their heads back and laughed? Well, how about you just suck it up and join in with the laughter, it's not really going to hurt anyone, is it?

Somewhere along the line it all got serious, people would phone up bloody radio programmes and would say they resented being portrayed as a bunch of skinflint bastards in their city because they themselves are from a suburb of that city and give to charity regularly and know loads of people in their street who are anything but tight with their money, others would say that a joke was really out of date about their town being cultureless because these people making the jibes obviously didn't know about the new Cultural Centre For Culture that had been purpose built in the city centre next to the Regional Art Gallery of Regional Art that people definitely visited in huge numbers and it definitely wasn't a white elephant despite what people in the popular press are saying who clearly are wanting to do this great place down.

My argument with most types of stereotyping isn't the idea that people are stereotyping per se, rather it is that it comes from people who have no fucking clue about the people they're sending up.

As a lad with a Scottish father but brought up in an outpost in the far North of England with its own identity, I find English jingoism hilarious at times. I used to get angry about it, then after trying to silently empathise with these people on a patronising level, I then just took the view that these people weren't even worth wasting listening time to and nowadays I just shake my head whenever I hear an idiot talking about how they think the Celts behave and try to understand their actions because they're in some way jealous of their English masters.

We live in a fucked up country that has always jarred with itself due mainly to rampant capitalism that has invariably required a huge labour force being needed in a hurry, therefore people arrive by the shit load to cope with demand, those people are normally housed in the worst parts of town where it's the cheapest rent, and they tend to live next others from that part of the world, hence ghettos and places dubbed 'little Ireland' or 'Jerusalem' etc.

Long before Eastern Europeans coming over en masse 20 years ago and of course Indians, Bangladeshis and Pakistanis getting across to the UK in the 60s and 70s and West Indians from the Empire Windrush from 1948 onwards, the main immigrants were the Irish. Obviously they were from large families, and rightly or wrongly their largely rural country where they came from wouldn't have had any infrastructure or advanced technology and their education would be at a very basic level. Hence a lot of naïve things being said as they worked in Victorian factories where stuff would be churned out very quickly through a combination of compressed steam power and tool slides transferring rotary motion to linear motion and vice versa. 'Sure there must be a little man in there working that' would maybe have been the initial observations, hence 'thick paddies' and the like. Obviously only until recent years do you have lobbies against stereotyping, but for 200 years the daily fayre would have been how dense the Irish people were at work and no one would have challenged the alleged perpetrators.

My Scottish father said that he was called a 'tight jock bastard' and a 'typical dour Scot' and other unpleasantries pretty much every day at his work. On other occasions different people would hurl the same insult but it was meant to be what they call these days 'banter', probably because the latter group were his friends. His nation of birth was belittled and sneered at and was the object of scorn at work during independence campaigns, World Cups and whenever there was Scottish buffoonery taking place in British showbusiness like Neil Reid, The Bay City Rollers or Lena Zavaroni. He said that he just took it at whatever level it was intended, he didn't feel the need to take people to court or feel that he was having his dignity and with it his human rights stripped away because someone laughed at Alan Rough's antics or sang the chorus to Shangalang in a silly voice while he was trying to go through a shift rota.

Do you hate xenophobic humour? Do you feel that a country

should be put through the ringer by people during their working day? It's not for me to answer for you and no one is right and no one is wrong, but honestly if you think that there's too many sheep jokes about your land of birth, or too many one liners about their fondness for drink when their government are really trying hard to shake off that image, then maybe planet Earth in the human years aren't for you.

THE STAND-UP'S LICENCE

It's great how people call us philosophers, that people see us as the Socrates and Plato of our days. The older I get the more I feel it's just the poetry-like timing and the preparation to find a good apt word in the right circumstance that makes someone funny. The idea that comedians can see things from the angles that others don't is just one of those great myths in life.

I do love it when we get escalated to this Zen-like level of wisdom when some middle class silly-billy parades around a shiny floor with a radio mic on late night television gleefully telling us that his wife decides on what groceries they get in Sainsbury's and that the stuff he chooses gets hastily put back on the shelf — "well we won't be needing those" he shouts, mimicking his pain in the arse wife's voice to the ending of days laughter of recognition from the paying audience, then a hastily thrown together round of applause for good measure of an observation that mere mortals like them just couldn't have thought of. By the way that isn't any comedian in particular that I'm quoting from, but it could be scores of them.

Most comedians do the opposite that they're supposed to do, in my opinion. Instead of people going away saying 'that's right we do do that, don't we', people end up just getting their stereotypes reinforced and keeping in mind the same thoughts that they already had about early 21st century domestic life within the UK. Punk is long, long dead; in fact I sometimes think it never even happened.

I remember the great Tony Law on stage in Edinburgh at The Stand Comedy Club during the Fringe. The Fringe in case anyone doesn't know is the biggest arts festival in the world and it takes place in Edinburgh, the capital of Scotland, every August. Amongst the plays and revues as well as one man/one woman shows and singer/songwriters along with ghost hunts, Shakespeare companies and musical recitals, children's shows and lots more, there's literally hundreds of stand-up comedians doing an hour of stuff in different rooms all over the city for three and a half weeks. Anyway, the Stand club is in the new town, not as manic as the old town for the month, but maybe populated with older, more discerning punters. Tony, during his show, said that his hour might be different to what you might see over the other side of town with all the young comics that 'notice things'. I think most people in the crowd knew what he meant, the idea that this banal level of observation represented high art and a footnote in comedy history is risible to say the fucking least. Also, everyone else is observing so you getting on stage and observing almost makes it like an observational Olympics. The trouble is critics were getting fooled by this, constantly hailing these haircut buffoons as the next Connolly or the next Izzard or the next Jesus Christ, such was the plot losing in some of these reviews when these young chaps in the words of Tony 'noticed things'.

"Shout out a subject and I'll do a joke about it" was one comedian's ultimate claim. I worked with this person a lot on the circuit back in the day and this line was wheeled out at different parts of the set depending upon the night in question. I'm sure he wasn't the first or the last comedian to do this, but the deluded level of arrogance was mind blowing. Obviously as you can imagine the works of EM Forster or post-war West Bromwich Albion teams didn't come up, instead drunken shouts of 'Sex', 'fucking drugs' or how the nearby town was apparently full of twats. Some of the pseudo intellectuals would shout out 'the government' or something so vague that he could freewheel to anywhere on the political spectrum and have maintained the self set remit.

Of course, I do understand that stand-up comedy and the art of making a room full of drinkers laugh is not about high art. I'm also not a snob, it's great on its night, it kicks the shit out of the cinema, the theatre, Ted talks or any form of opera for its immediacy and rawness and its ability to break down a fourth wall, but it is what it is, it's a bit of late night fun with a few pints. Would you like it to be anything more than that? I wouldn't personally because then we've lost Billy Connolly, Victoria Wood, Jasper Carrott and Lee Mack and all their great routines and daft one-liners. They'd have been replaced many years ago by some of the sort of people I've worked with down the years, the ones that try and exhume the art of stand-up comedy and do a post-mortem on it and explain how banal it all is. The dissectors of comedy never thought of one funny idea themselves; they just stood in the milky twilight and harrumphed at it. If you spend time with some of these people after the show you lose the will to live; thank God they didn't get the keys to the comedy van. I tell you this though, the powers that be in TV and radio land would have fought tooth and nail to have the airwaves completely populated by these faldy daldy types, I guarantee you that. I wouldn't put Stewart Lee in this bracket as he sort of does it tongue in cheek and is brilliant at it. His pretend infallibility comes over and most people realise that he's smug and self satisfied deliberately to get a rise out of people, and his conceitedness is sort of self fulfilling as in people want to see him being even more of a heartless twat than he already is. Of course there are psueds out there that don't get the irony of it all, but that's the spoils of war.

As stand-ups I think we're allowed to say that all bus drivers and doctor's receptionists are miserable, we're allowed to mimic the voice of the fuckwit woman serving you your cup of tea and ham sandwich in a café in the market; similarly we're allowed to make the right-on woman that works as equality officer at Lambeth council a silly fucker with a monotone plummy accent, we're allowed to make the builders a bit sexist and the doctor a bit condescending. They're clichés but they're clichés that are part of the game. What we do is bawdy entertainment and kitchen sink humour in a lot of cases, we're not there for historical accuracy — nobody ever looked at the works of music hall comedian and early member of The Grand Order Of Water Rats Dan Leno to find out what life was really like in Victorian Britain; he was an entertainer and that's what we do, entertain.

I've noticed that in old music hall comedians' routines like Max Miller and in the more modern variety era Roy Chubby Brown, the doctor in many of their bawdy jokes always tends to be male and is very often a bit of a lech who has subtly got to get a look at his wife's private parts or there are suggestions that the doctor has done something depraved or managed to con his missus into having sex with him, an example being Roy Chubby Brown 'you know that trouble that I was having with my minge, the doctor says he's got it licked'. Of course it's a play on words and it is very funny, but it implies that the doctor was thinking of any way to get a go on Chubby's wife even if it was to fix a gynaecological condition.

I've heard many a rumour of GPs having sex with their patients from hearsay to alleged FACT!! Sorry, that's a call back to an earlier chapter. However, I'm sure the vast majority don't have sex with their patients and would laugh off the accusation. It's not appropriation though, it's just a bit of fun.

Also as a comic, logic always applies, but it's how you apply the logic in the story that you're telling in the first person. If you're at your wit's end with council red tape and all the procedures and hoop jumping that you have to partake in to speak to the right person on the phone, your story has to bring out how you were going stir crazy being put on hold and that everyone was a bit of a fool in the various departments that you spoke to and that you were the voice of reason and you're bringing the audience on this journey of you trying to keep your cool in this world that apparently is going mad. In stand-up comedy these days, particularly with men it's always the stand-ups themselves that are the straight men in their stories and everyone else within the establishment or those that work for the man are the idiots, and they want the audience to be on their side as a result.

Sadly, these days it appears that stand-up comedy is being hijacked, it's definitely being hijacked in part by the right wing — probably this has a lot to do with people on the other side of the spectrum having no bloody sense of humour whatsoever and therefore we have a natural reaction taking place. The sad part of it all though is that these people with 'agendas' are the antithesis of comedy because they have no sense of irony or sardony, or an ability to burst out laughing at their own political and idealistic shortcomings, or if they do they immediately feel that the joke on them has to be 'balanced out' with a joke about the other side but the joke to compensate for their minor foibles has to be a one where a point is hammered home as to what a bunch of cunts their enemies are just so we all know what side they're on.

For those of us of a certain age, we had loads of examples

of the alleged freedom fighting opposition Labour Party that seemed to be an opposition party forever, telling us about the dreadful government and taking part in loads of dreadful satirical sketches and going on the TV chat show circuit pummelling the then Conservative government with their barbed tongue. They were all at it, Kaufman, Hattersley, Kinnock, Smith, Brown, Prescott, Beckett, Cook, Straw, Harman and then later Blair of course. The irony of course was that these blokes and women, once they'd taken the Conservatives' place in 1997 and got their feet under the table behaved exactly as a Tory party would and nothing changed, we all continued to live in this low paid, low skilled, low tax, service industry economy that made the rich get richer, only now they had fancy words like 'new deal', 'sure start', 'assisted places' and 'education, education, education' that they liked to trumpet, which tried to soften the blow of more conservatism. However, they weren't keen to parrot phrases like 'private finance initiative' or 'tuition fees', you know the things that showed them for the scummy fuckers that they actually were.

The soundbite and the use of satire for one's political ends takes away the anarchic sketch group or the free spirit stand-up comedian that doesn't give a fuck. As soon as you find that the Democrats in America are signing up Sarah Silverman, whom I thought was a terrific loose cannon comedian, you realise that all bets are off. When you watch an old 'roast' (I can't stand those fucking things by the way) of Don Rickles the American comedian who apparently was a lifelong Democrat taking apart Republican Ronald Reagan sometime in the 80s while he's in the audience but saying nice stuff at the end means that these people aren't jazz maestros or not giving a fuck merchants, but rather very much part of the staid conservative establishment and not on the fringes as they claim to be.

FORMATIVE
YEARS

SCHOOL

Of course school is where you learn to interact. For me it was a place that you learned stuff from the teachers, but more importantly you learned about the pack, about what people liked, about how to interact in a group, and in my case I found out exactly what early to mid-1970s culture was like when I started and what mid-80s culture was when I left, and saw all the changes in between despite being a kid. Remember, you take in loads at that age and I was always observant about the way people behaved. In our early years we tend to listen to a confident bullshitter. I remember a kid in my infant school (they weren't called primary schools back then) showing me the ropes as it were but thinking back now he was younger than me so must have started on exactly the same day or maybe even after me, but his confidence was palpable and I was in awe of this sage telling me the dos and don'ts of school life. "When you hear that noise you've got to run," he said. The noise in question was a steel bin being kicked. It was in the sheds so it must have made the acoustics sting the air because to a four year old it was very loud. For months, maybe a year, I would suddenly pick up a sprint whenever I heard that sound and it took me many years to twig that the kid in question was just talking out of his young arse. He's high up in Northumbria Police now, the last time I saw him was on a motorway service station on the M62 heading to Liverpool to orchestrate a drugs bust so maybe there is a lineage somewhere between confident young liar to DI Cantsayhisname!

During my young years I was told all sorts of things by liars with confidence and I believed pretty much everything, but that's allowed. When we're young we are vying for position and not entirely sure who we are so along the way we're taken in by types who love to embellish stories (see the first chapter).

Wikipedia killed the bullshitter is a phrase that I'll trot out throughout the book (actually maybe I won't) and just as 'Video Killed The Radio Star' according to The Buggles in their 1979 hit (also the first record played on MTV, ironic that these music television stations are in real trouble these days and radio is still going strong), it's true that a veritable trivia facts information service that's 99.99% accurate has taken the brass balls away from the confident bloke in the pub that swears that he's right.

When I was about 14, I used to hang around with a right pair of thick cunts that lived in my street. There was no choice really, the slightly older kids in my estate were getting off with the lasses and underage drinking, we had nothing in common with the younger lads and my mates from school lived a bus ride away, and back in the early 80s that was like going to an area of the occupied West Bank so it was easier to suffer the lack of stimulating conversation with the dead beats from the bottom of the estate than go on a Marco Polo type adventure to a different housing estate altogether with different customs and rules and a different corner shop to visit.

These two lads were never wrong, they declared me 'thick' – this was despite evidence to the contrary, namely being in higher sets than them at school – however, such is one's lack of confidence at that age I thought that I must be thick compared to them because apparently I knew fewer things so to speak. Looking back at it now, they clearly had more brash and altogether streetwise parents. Maybe my father was just as streetwise as both their fathers as a bloke who'd done his national service in the Royal Navy and got into all sorts of adventures in different ports around the world and then spent years living on his own in Newcastle as a bachelor after coming down from Scotland before he got settled and married, but their dads by the sound of it went to work and probably brought the harsh, dogmatic factory floor speak home to the tea table and that's where both boys learnt their concise practical factfinding and blunt speak, very much the epitome of this book. My father, on the other hand, wanted to tell me about the bigger picture and taught me to look outward; theirs was very inward.

Enough of the sociology speak though, I remember one time

when they got talking about population and how many people lived in our hometown of Blaydon. I told them that according to my dad's RAC book the population of Blaydon was 14,500. If you check Wikipedia now it says that the current population is 15,155 so that was probably about right back then (this would be about 1983-84). Well I was laughed out of court — 'fuck off, 14 and a half thousand?! There's about 300 on our estate on its own'! I said that that's what it said in the book and they just carried on 'goes to show how thick you are, what about all the other streets on the estate and look at the rows of houses on Blaydon bank and the Bronx (the nickname for the really rough council estate) as well as all the estates in Winlaton'. After hammering home the point and reminding me how stupid I was I came back with 'Well what would you say Blaydon's population was?' — their answer: 'I'd say it must be about 100,000', then the other kid threw in the immortal line 'at least'! And sure enough not to disappoint the first kid concurred 'aye at least'. I couldn't let this go and said, 'So you're saying Blaydon has a population of 100,000, the whole of Newcastle has a population of less than 300,000, so you're saying Blaydon is a third of the size of Newcastle?' Their answer: 'Oooooh, Newcastle's a lot bigger than 300,000, it must be a couple of million.'

'At least!'

'Aye at least!'

It's at that point I stopped arguing and realised that the best thing to do was stay silent and let their deluded levels of intellect remain in their psyche. It's them who will have been ridiculed in the future for biting off more than they can chew by sitting with people of a much higher intellectual level and trying, yet of course failing, to outdo them – we've all seen that and it all starts in the teenage years by being ignorant but being blissfully aware that they are.

By the way, the way that story got concluded satisfactorily that day, certainly in the mind of the main protagonist sitting on his Raleigh Grifter at the time and embracing the fact that little Blaydon on Tyne had a population of six figures was that where I had gone wrong was that the 14,500 that I'd read was the amount of people WHO BOUGHT THE RAC BOOK that lived in Blaydon! I'm chuckling as I type this thinking back!! Ha ha, imagine if the RAC handbook sold 14 and a half thousand in a small suburb of Gateshead. Basically, by the reckoning of that, the 1981 RAC handbook will have sold something in the region of 55 and a half million, the population of the United Kingdom at that time. Fuck me, talk about best sellers!! It knocks the King James Bible or Pilgrims Progress off the top spot instantly and would be the biggest literary phenomenon of all time. Honestly, what a dense bastard! Christ only knows how many the AA handbook sold!! I wonder when the penny ever dropped, or perhaps he forgot about his diatribe maybe even the next week – that's probably the most likely scenario.

The kid in question did a few thick arsed things, which to be fair this book, as you know, isn't about. He once confidently claimed that Stranraer was on the east side of Scotland and I insisted it was on the west side of Scotland and when an atlas was shown to him he said 'Aye it's on the west going up and on the east coming down'. Also, he once went straight over the cable with my dad's lawnmower citing that he didn't think he'd snap the cable because 'it doesn't do that on the adverts'! Yes, a silly cunt it goes without saying, but the population thing was one of those classic cases of I'm right, you're talking shit and you can't prove me wrong. I'm a fan of population, I have been since I was a kid; it's the autistic side of me. I knew even as an awkward teenager that I was right on this occasion but the empty vessel making the most noise won and his not as loud but equally confident mate endorsed him all the way. If Wikipedia was around now that argument would've been put straight to bed, and they would have had to argue that they were right about something more niche or nuanced which might have been beyond their 'Daily Mirror Book of Facts' type education they were getting in home as well as school.

A mate of mine was in a taxi in Bristol once and asked the taxi driver what the population of Bristol was. 'Oh I dunno,' the driver said in his Vicky Pollard accent, 'Nine, Ten million.' Maybe the taxi driver had spent his life smirking at quieter people that said to him that he might have overestimated that and that Bristol's population was more like half a million, or maybe it was a shot in the dark; either way it was probably something someone said to him at school and it's stuck without him ever challenging the facts by using a bit of common sense. Or more than likely he said to the more thoughtful kid 'Half a million?! There's five people in my house and that's only one house'!!

Speaking of Bristol, I remember a wonderful debate involving another ill-informed mouthpiece on late night 5 Live, this particular one was from the BNP back when they had a flurry of support during the noughties. It was all about immigration and the numbers of people coming over here making Britain their new home. The debate involved him, a couple of liberal minded people from some puffed up organisation who thought that all immigration was great (you know the usual BBC thing of fanatics debating stuff that perversely doesn't represent the majority of the listeners' views) and the writer and critic David Quantick. It ebbed and flowed one way and the other and the presenter was trying his best to be the devil's advocate when it wasn't really needed as every silly comment on either side was covered. Anyway, charmless BNP man said that it really was worrying because there are half a million immigrants coming over every year and (here is the quote) "there are cities the size of Bristol needing to be built every year to cope with the demand". After he'd said his piece and the rah rah right ons had had their say, the presenter turned to David Quantick and asked him what he made of it all and if he was in favour of mass immigration. Quantick's reply was measured but stinging. He said: "Well first of all I'd like to know where all these cities the size of Bristol are, are they underwater?" It's very rare that I laugh out loud especially on my own, but that was one of those moments.

THE
WORLD
OF
WORK

SEEING THE WORST IN PEOPLE

The first place anyone gets disappointed with the world and the people in it, in my opinion, is when you start work. Whether that be when you're cleaning tables in tea rooms in town for the blue rinse women, or when you walk into an office or a call centre aged 16 as a junior, or when you land a job in a warehouse or get thrown in at the deep end at Sainsbury's. Your first job has no filter, there's no schoolteachers saying "right let's do that again, Abbey, you be the shopkeeper now, Erin can be the angry customer", or a college instructor calling a halt to the role playing and when they do continue all the 'ways to do it wrong' are so effete and not of the real world. I didn't know what I was letting myself in for when I started work but I'm so glad looking back that I did go to work when I was 16 because I seemed to grow up immediately and see the worst in people.

I naively thought that all foremen, gaffers and factory floor managers had been on some sort of course on how to deal with people and employees and knew the art of diplomacy and compromise as well as how to lead people, and this was all through vital information passed down from older managers as well as the studying of books on the subject. This was probably due to my birth in that by the mid-1980s we were all being signed up for courses like a City and Guilds in Communication and BTECs in Customer Relations etc, very much the world we're living in now but back then just in its infancy. These fears were augmented when I worked in a factory in Darlington and the foreman (an angry nasty bloke called Kenny) had a load of books in his office area with titles like 'Leadership' and 'The Art of Management', that sort of thing. They were thick hardback books and stood back-to-back on his shelf alongside micrometres, verniers and other small technical equipment. As I gradually worked it out although it took me a long time because I was young and green he'd never even looked at these bloody books, they were just sat proudly on his shelf for show and they'd been accrued from previous managers and foremen at the factory that were there years, even generations ago. As time went on it became clear that the bloke was almost illiterate and hadn't read a book in his life let alone a deep psychological one about the relationship between peers in the mid 20th century (they were clearly quite old books even for the late 80s). His lack of getting the best out of people was palpable as he just shouted and bullied his way through the day and was a useless foreman. He eventually got sacked because whilst working on a job, a precision job making instruments to temporarily widen railway tracks, he cut corners, and in order to get them out on time, he conveniently 'forgot' to case harden the steel pins that went inside the wood that supported its spring mechanism. He sort of hoped they wouldn't check on the thing that was of the most importance, you know the thing that underpinned what they were doing for health and safety when some blokes are working on a death trap like a railway line! Needless to say, he was fired instantly as the components were sent back and I presume the firm weren't asked to make any more.

Maybe the working world has changed now and there aren't any Kennys left running factories making vital components to keep people safe and it's finely tuned and skilled, well-read people that are clued up in the art of management in his place, but I suspect not. Have a look who's running the country and give me an honest punt on whether this may the case?!!

A comedian I worked with quite regularly then supported on his first tour, who is now quite famous, was being very decent to people. He was getting more famous as the tour went on and his decency was almost at odds with the exponential way his fame was growing. He got talking to a homeless person once in a fairly small town and invited him to one of his shows. The next time he was in said town (I was in the venue ready to do the support) the homeless man was demanding he come into the theatre as a guest because said comic had promised him. The security had a right job stopping him getting in. They said the comedian wanted to go and talk to him but this was not advised. The comedian's dad who was there said that the trouble with *********** is that he's young and he always just sees the best in people.

Now on the surface that sounds quite depressing in that he was implying that he just needs to get older to realise that there's an awful lot of cunts out there, and he'll learn that and in turn will do fuck all for anyone and then everything will be okay. However, I could see the dad's point.

Anyone brought up in this country post-war has had to protect what they had and be wary of others because there's a lot of people who would just rob off you and try and fuck you over, then when after 1979 being selfish and dropping others in the shit was positively encouraged by the state, it heightened those tensions right up. Yes, it's a miserable thought but seeing the best in people does spell trouble. What a great country, eh?!!

When I worked in various factories on Tyneside and County Durham from the mid-80s to the early 90s I met a lot of people. Well I'll rephrase that, I met a lot of blokes, that's right, blokes, blerks, blurkes, gadgeys, blokies, blokes, lots and lots of them. They ranged from dashing good looking blokes (quite rare) to fucking mutants with overalls on. These were the sort of blokes you didn't think existed and I'm certain they didn't exist outside of these places. Red faced, wild hair, bad breath, nasal hair poking from areas other than the nose, fuck and cunt in every sentence, very frequently extolling the virtues of pounding the living shit out of good looking young women in the public eye and in speaking in a blasé way about it in that they genuinely thought they stood a good chance of having a quick one with Linda Lusardi or Anneka Rice should they be passing by Shitty-Balls Engineering one Wednesday afternoon when the boss was away out in the van. They were obsessed with finding out which one of the apprentices/ YTS kids was still a virgin, then the ritual piss taking would commence, you know high end stuff like 'so are you sure you're not a bender then?' or 'imagine her (normally a Page 3 woman) being left for five minutes with Craig/Lee/Paul, he wouldn't even know what to do!'. This was then followed by riotous laughter and a follow up comment along the lines of 'I was shagging owt that moved when I was your age, son'.

They used to encourage me to join in, which I reluctantly did at first but then realised that they were braggarts with a pound of bullshit thrown in. All I remember thinking about these fuckers was that the late 1950s and early 1960s in the North East of England just seemed like some sort of rape fest full of these hideous blokes a generation and a half younger on the prowl, and I retrospectively pitied the young women of the time.

No wonder middle aged women in my adolescence were so full of disdain for young people and all the trappings of 1980s life, I mean the poor buggers had to spend their youth giving in to these Neanderthalic men and then reluctantly marrying one of the bastards to keep her safe from a mod or a rocker, or worse still one of the ban the bomb brigade with a duffle coat on, or a West Indian or a queer or something.

Anyway, these blokes, when they weren't talking about rough

but consensual sex with a very keen Anne Diamond or Kim Wilde, used to patronise the fuck out of you with their politics. Looking back, they were all over the place with their views even though they convinced you they were very consistent with them. Lots of them were Labour voters, in fact 90% of them were Labour voters. They stuck up for the miners and hated Thatcher. The fact was in 1986, the year long strike of 84-85 was still very much in the British psyche, it was still raw and the Conservatives still had a lot to do to capture the hearts and minds of the British people. Indeed, it would take that great Conservative Tony Blair (some 10 years later) to get people to at last not give a fuck and finally shit completely on their own folk and divorce themselves from their own brethren that just happened to be more down on their luck than them when the hedonistic 90s hit.

'Aye Thatcher, stupid cow', 'Tell you what, give me five minutes with that witch, I'd take her head clean off with an axe' and so on and so forth. The ways of killing her were so hatstand and bizarre it was as if she was a cartoon character – 'just an axe, Davey? I'd strip her naked, tickle her with a feather duster then stick a broom handle up her arse so far so it's coming out of her mouth and then roast her on an open spit', 'to be honest what I'd do is...' on and on ad infinitum.

The caveat to all that though is that they were nearly all massively racist, unknowingly sexist, and gay people were figures of fun in their eyes. I remember I worked for Harrison's Brushes, a firm that designed and assembled industrial and domestic brushes. The foreman didn't like me much, mainly because I think he thought they were trying to get me to take his job. He was very reluctant to show me how things worked and would part with information about the ins and outs of the machines like he was giving his worst card away in a seedy game of poker. He'd deliberately race through explaining to me how to set a machine up so I wouldn't get it first time and when I asked him again he'd say stuff like "I thought you would've picked this up by now?". Anyway, that's setting the scene. Basically, he was looking after himself and no one else. He ridiculed a mammy's boy type kid there for the usual reason, the fact that he was 18 and hadn't had his end away yet, he didn't like an older gadgey that worked there probably because the bloke was properly time served and he wasn't, and there was disdain for anyone else that he saw was a threat.

Anyway, he was all for Labour, saying that back in the day when there were Labour governments you had plenty of money in your pocket and you were looked after and no one was out to get you, the unions protected you and things cost less. It was like the buzzing of the bees and the cigarette trees and the soda water fountains. It was explained to me in such a patronising way about how the great times had been crushed by this devil in a blue dress. The irony of all this was that he was the epitome of Thatcherism, I'm fucking alright Jack and if any bastard gets in my way I'll cry to management and snitch on the fuckers for not working hard enough or not understanding the job so they'll get written warnings and I'll keep rolling along as production manager. He did this with me and several others, several times.

Of course, to contradict this wistful look at the past when everyone in the working classes supposedly had the safety net well and truly installed by the great Labour Party, he would say awful things about immigrants. It was always primeval and antediluvian — 'Why should we do owt for them? They're all monkeys, man', 'I tell you what, I'd do nowt for a darkie or a paki, would they do owt for us? Would they fuck'.

I remember him telling me about Enoch Powell in glowing terms and how his idea to send all the Darkies back home got him loads of votes and everyone thought he was great. Yes, these were the people I worked with! The great thing was that these blokes assumed that you wouldn't have a clue who Enoch Powell was let alone know what he was infamous for, and he could embellish his way through it and make the story sound like some sort of industrial backdrop, kitchen sink fairy-tale. Also, what I was too polite to point out to him as a fairly bashful 19-year-old was that Enoch Powell was in fact a Tory politician and cabinet member not from this wonderful Labour Party that he was espousing.

I didn't last too long at Harrison's Brushes — the management didn't think I was working too hard, no doubt prompted by the Enoch-loving foreman having a quiet word. I knew I had to jump before I was pushed and fortunately I got offered a job back in the previous horrible engineering firm I'd worked for that had moved to a massive factory nearer where I lived. That was full of racists as well, but it was bigger and you could spring from one racist to another throughout the miserable day, rather than be stuck with just one badly educated bigot in a small industrial unit.

Are all racists bad? In my view I'd say they were. To have a prejudice just over the colour of a skin is ludicrous, isn't it?

WHAT'S IN A TITLE?

"The wife's packing everything into the carrier bag, she shouts up the stairs 'Bobby, the handle's snapped on the carrier' whey I'm not an engineer" – Bobby Thompson.

The great Bobby Thompson getting it spot on there in the guise of a domestic observation. The belittlement of a multi-layered profession but in an indirect way. I'm an engineer myself, I did five and a half years in factories, I didn't get an indentured apprenticeship but I did do a City and Guilds in Basic engineering competences at Newcastle College, a welding certificate at Tyne Met, then a City and Guilds in CAD design at Gateshead College, all in the evenings while working in the day time, followed by two years full time at Sunderland Polytechnic doing an HND in Mechanical and Manufacturing Engineering. We had to do a main project which was long and laborious and took months for us to complete, and I had to work it with someone else, but also I had to pass modules like fluid engineering, instrumentation and mechanics which were maths and physics based right through to communications which entailed writing arduous and turgid essays about works relations and how to deal with workforces. At the end you do feel fulfilled because I felt that when I came out of college and back into the world of work, well, I should say the job market again, I felt that despite not being a born engineer, I was still an engineer and no one could take that away from me. Now imagine someone washing your car at the car wash and pressing a few buttons calling themselves a car wash engineer?!! Have you seen that? I have. It was big in the 90s to get a token from the garage and put it in the slot but to leave your engine off and put it in neutral so 'one of our engineers can take it from there'! These people were happy to tell you down the pub that they were engineers and that electric car washes were what they were erm... er... engineers in.

It doesn't stop there: you get your Indesit washing machine fixed (other makes are available), like getting the pump replaced by someone who comes out and charges a fortune but you can't do it yourself because it's not covered on the warranty and the fixtures and fittings are made from some kind of Narnia spec so you can't get your own tools in them and he calls himself or herself an 'engineer'. All they happen to be are people who know an Indesit back to front and nowt else. I don't have a problem with what they get paid or how good or cushy their job is, good luck to them, it's just the fact that they happily call themselves engineers despite never once attending even a night class to know the first thing about the history of screws, threads, centre lathes, Whitworth or Henry Maudslay.

My late father (I'm sure he wasn't the first to observe this) said that people were given fancy titles by their boss and it kept them quiet about asking for more money. A fancy job title basically could justify you not being paid very well. I remember my last casual job before I went into the comedy world full time was as a driver for a car hire company; me and someone else would go in two cars and one of us would drop the car off at an address and then they would be given a lift to another address where the driver would pick one up that had come off hire and then said driver would follow you in that car to the one you dropped off and they would pick you up and you'd both go back to the depot for the next job. The drivers (mainly retired blokes but various other people as well, students, people wanting a second job income and various other waifs and strays) were quite literally the driving force in the job. We were out there getting the cars to people on time and there to sort out queries and take credit card payments while out at private addresses or big businesses. We were just drivers though; nothing more, nothing less. Some of the older blokes had been employed with major companies in the past and had done well for themselves but they were now just drivers getting the job done.

The people in the office assigning us jobs were just the people receiving orders and then deciding about how we could all get the job done quickly and efficiently by pairing drivers up and seeing as to what part of Tyne and Wear, County Durham and Northumberland we should be heading out to and in what order. Invariably they were a bit shit at it and just anally went through the jobs by seeing names of towns coming up on their computer screen. For example, if they saw four jobs come up in Sunderland so they would send two drivers to Sunderland to do all of those jobs; however, another set of two drivers would get a job in the north west of County Durham then another one in South Durham and then two in North East Durham, racking up a nigh on 100 mile round trip all told. Now Durham is a big county and the Sunderland drivers could easily have picked up the North East Durham jobs because they weren't far away from it being that North East Durham is just south of the city of Sunderland. No foresight whatsoever. Also, Tyneside in case anyone doesn't know, is an east to west conurbation separated by a river. If some job was way out west where the Tyne is so narrow you could practically jump over it, a job north or south of the Tyne wouldn't really make much difference – the same drivers could swing across and take pick up or drop off in Wylam (north of the Tyne) if they were together doing a job in Crawcrook (south of the Tyne). This fairly straightforward detail was beyond some of the people in the office and you had a farcical situation of two different sets of drivers doing different pick ups and drop offs within a stone's throw of each other. We were nearly always on time but when we were unavoidably late due to not being able to get there on time due to our last job being many miles away, the office would just blame the drivers; you'd have an irate person asking where you'd been and then when you explained they told you that the office had said you were on your way an hour ago.

These people that gave us our daily jobs though were known as 'Fleet managers', then there were the 'Fleet assistant managers' but nothing else. Not one of them was a fleet office worker, they were all just 'managers' and in front of house there were 'Sales and Hire managers', it seemed like everyone in the office was a manager or an assistant manager. The old phrase 'too many chiefs and not enough Indians' was very much evident on this occasion. To square the circle, I found out how much they were paid as everyone who has worked will know that people's salaries get leaked all over the place, you can't keep quiet about what you get paid in the world of work, it's almost sacrilege. Needless to say it was a fucking pittance, but you can bet your boots the exclusively young people that were employed as 'Fleet managers' and 'Sales and hire managers' would be full of it, telling their circle of friends, neighbours they didn't like to get one up on the bastards, or their Aunty Maureen at Christmas, that they had these highfalutin job titles which was the watchword or the currency for 'doing well'. When you were late for a job because you were somewhere else in the county half an hour ago while someone else couldn't take it that was a few streets away due to a chronic lack of geographical knowledge mixed with common sense from a 'manager', then you totally understood why they were paid crappy money. I must remember if I ever employ someone to give them a dynamic title.

SHOWBUSINESS

I'm in showbusiness. I've been in showbusiness for a long time, 29 years or so and 24 full time. Believe you me, 24 years in showbusiness is gold clock territory. Anyone can tap dance for a summer season or be a keyboard player in a piss poor covers band that were getting bookings for 18 months but now they've dried up and you have to go back to driving a van; however, to still troop the boards doing the same thing you'd set out to do when you started for 15 or 20 plus years takes that special something. You have to have persistence and you have to dig deep. You have to be able to shrug your shoulders when something that promised so much fades away to dust and you have to develop a self effacing sense of humour. It's all going to look embarrassing and the worst decision you ever made joining this circus and crying with clown's make up on is much more of a kick in the teeth than wearing a suit at the bank and having a quivering lip.

The attention hoggers and self obsessed that indulge daily on social media with the 'humblebrag' don't last. The reason they don't last? Really good self-obsessed twats are busy with their next dastardly move to conquer the world, not wanking themselves off about how good they are on Facebook. Also, the career minded 'humbled and proud' types that tell us that they've got some showbiz job that they want to think that everyone reading it would've wanted, have no sense of humour or irony, they can't send themselves up or belittle their own arrogance — these traits are quite essential for stand-up comedy, don't you think?

In the post alternative comedy circuit, the first lot were the satirists, my generation were the hedonists and the new set of comedians are definitely the careerists. The thing about careers rather than attractions is that a career ends and in showbusiness it ends quietly. The old adage of 'you never leave showbusiness, showbusiness leaves you' is such a good one but it's always a one that hurts when I hear it even though it hasn't happened to me yet. I think it's the anticipation and dread of when it may happen. The quite prophetic part of our job is that whenever a name comes up from the past, it's always followed by a 'bloody hell I forgot about him, I wonder what he's doing now', or 'last thing I heard about her was that she'd gone on a joinery course and was making cupboards'. The stage, much like other industries but with more epic grandiose-ness is a case of when you're in you're in but when your time is gone no one gives a solitary fuck, you might as well be dead. Wikipedia I think was invented for people to find out what footballers did for the 40 years after people stopped being bothered about them.

I, like people in my industry that have been around for years because none of us suffers fools gladly, get taken in by ambitious young agents. If one of these young bucks says without irony 'stick with me and I'll get you on the telly' you just laugh at their naivety — believe it or not we still get those comments thrown at us along with 'don't you want to be famous?' or 'age and discrimination is not a barrier, not working hard enough is', yes we've had all those beauts in our time. There are those out there, normally the ones who buy them silly books you can buy in airports called something like 'The 7 Different Steps To Being King Fucking Biscuit' are the very ones that think that negative thinking is only what is standing in people's ways of getting on and that positivity moves mountains. The fact is that showbusiness is like everything, it's a cruel game and although it is largely a meritocracy, it's not an absolute science — right place right time is not a cliché for nothing and if you're hanging round in the one place for too long the buses all leave and you're left behind.

I still get a kick out of the fact I'm in showbusiness, I still like the idea. I like the idea of it because as an industry it's fucking ludicrous, it's kind of silly and the sillier the idea the more chance that you could pull in a fortune or become a footnote in entertainment history, which to me is everything. It's like you've made the rules up as to what people like, who doesn't like that idea?!? I'm not a fan of saying something is hack or mainstream because everything that is the norm nowadays started out as a bananas idea from someone. It's not necessarily the same person that gets the riches is the one who thought of the original idea, but wherever you see benign bollocks on the telly, it's definitely the case that some people in a room came up with something they thought was bloody radical and probably too dangerous for the public to even contemplate that eventually got watered down into the pish you are watching on the box.

How many people say 'I never liked The Beatles, they were overrated' then they go on to tell you about a band that was supposedly much better? Bloody loads from the people I've met in my life but the irony that's always lost on them is that said band wouldn't have existed without The Beatles. The whole idea of a head up its own arse concept album wouldn't have existed without Sgt. Pepper's Lonely Hearts Club Band. The very thing people rip the piss out of started out as something radical and different at the time, but in general a lot of people can't see this. Is it a mental block or something? People can't seem to differentiate between different eras. People have difficulty relating morals and ideas as well as aspirations, inspirations and ambitions when they are looking at the 1970s and today. The 70s are now becoming 50 years old!! Of course, some of us remember it all like it was yesterday, but it still doesn't alter the fact that it was a long time ago. 'And people just let that sort of thing happen?!!' Yes, they did, mate, and why? Because times were different, that's why. Yes, we could debate for the rest of the week what was different and why it was different, but in short it was different so hence the different core values and expectation of what was right and what was wrong. You'd be amazed how many people just don't grasp this concept.

A well(ish) known comedian with a much more famous son was talking to a good mate of mine, probably my oldest mate in showbusiness (he himself is very well known and sells theatres out round the world and has done for many years due to his attraction as a unique act). The comedian was patronising my mate for not being accessible at the time to audiences for the improvised type stuff he did and warned him that he'd never find an audience doing what he was doing, yes the old this will never happen, guitar bands are on their way out schtick. How wrong he was, but I'm sure he wouldn't acknowledge his mistake now.

He said that the best way to get a crowd to like you was to get them to relate to what you're talking about. He maintained that what he himself was trying to achieve (with his safe, twee, married with 2.4 children, the price of prawns in Marks and Spencer's comedy) was to be the new Jasper Carrott, that was his exact words. My mate was discussing this with me and he pointed out quite correctly that the great Jasper Carrott was anything but the national treasure he is today when he first got into the public's consciousness. When he started in the folk clubs only beardy real ale drinkers would have been aware of him and then when he got himself a top 10 hit 'Funky Moped' in the mid 70s, it was said that the majority of people bought the record because of the B side 'The Magic Roundabout', a routine of his peppered with barely disguised innuendo and proper bad language (for the time) to boot. He was on television on 'An Audience With' long before it became mainstream, then in 1979 did a live show on ITV that had outrageous routines on it about local radio egotists, catching moles in his garden and the nutter sitting next to him on the bus shouting 'has anyone seen my camel?' – I remember this show on the night and me and my sister being allowed to watch it with my dad because my mother was out somewhere. As a show it really had an effect on me as a kid, here was a bloke not standing there in a suit with dickie bow tie saying 'I say, I say, I say' (honestly some comedians were still doing that back then, I'm not bullshitting), nor was he doing routines about fictional fellers going into a bar or holding up props or anything naff like that, he was a bloke with long hair and a lived-in face talking about life. He looked like one of the younger adults in my street, the ones that would have a bit of craic with the kids, not tell them to get off their wall or play at their own doors, and above all he was funny – I laughed out loud. There were kids I knew that used to ask me to recite the routines word for word to pass the time as we would spend days in the woods, or the burn, or walking a long distance, because it struck a chord with the young and no doubt teenagers as well. I guarantee there'd have been many letters of complaint to ITV for the bad language on that show and then when he got his own TV series Carrott's Lib in the early 80s I know for a fact that he got shit loads of complaints because I read them in my dad's Sunday papers – The Sunday Post (the semi religious but phenomenally popular Scottish Sunday paper that sold really well in the North East of England for some reason) seemed to have letters printed every week with anti-Carrott vitriol. Letters with all the usual clichés about this 'so called' comedian and lines like 'If he thinks he can get cheap laughs ridiculing the archbishop of Canterbury then he's not a good comedian' and 'laughing at the deaf just goes to show how far we've fallen with comedy' etc etc.

Over the years, as you know, Jasper Carrott has become very much loved by great swathes of the British public; he's almost up there with Billy Connolly as part of the nation's middle aged funny bone and defines an era in British comedy and a footnote in the history of comedy. To me he highlights the psyche of the British of a certain age, how we're vulnerable and hypocritical, and he shows us our greed and our insular attitudes at times, he definitely is someone to aspire to. However, you can't be Jasper Carrott straight away like said comedian wanted to be, you have to knock it out. He was public enemy number one to some back in the day, he wasn't liked by the older generation, probably for something simple like having long hair back in the 1970s, but also for his bawdy nature and brutal frankness about the way his lot (the baby boomer generation) were behaving. They didn't give a fuck to tell it like it was and the old bastards didn't like it. Now that the boomers ARE the old bastards, he has shone a light into how new generations aren't accepted at a time that isn't theirs but gradually are as they get older. The comedian might as well have said I intend to become the new Jesus Christ, not the bit where his people turn him over to the Romans to have him crucified, but rather thousands of years after his death when British colonials went round the world forcing people to worship him, yes that Jesus Christ era would be great.

OUTRAGE

'GO ON, YOU'VE GOT ANOTHER FIVE SECONDS, SAY SOMETHING OUTRAGEOUS' – BILL GRUNDY 1976

Oh yes, on December 1st, 1976 at around teatime, Britain almost instantly changed; you could argue that the Western world changed, but when you talk about sliding doors moments for this country this was definitely it. It wasn't as a result of war, a strike, a call to arms, something said in Parliament, a go slow or a sit in. People hadn't taken to the streets and there was no running battles with the coppers or the army; it was just a moment where the old guard got horrendously exposed.

It all took place on a quiet Wednesday at South Bank studios, London, on what was, I'm sure, just going to be a mundane slow news day in the capital, which in turn would churn out very much a knocked out edition of the London news, human interest and sport. Everyone that day was in for a shock. I might now sound like the cliché type people I keep describing in this book, but had this incident not happened then I don't think we'd be living in the same Britain that we do now, and I've yet to meet someone who can change my mind on that. I wouldn't care, the programme itself only went out in the London area, but when the then unknown (save for no more than a couple of hundred devotees) Sex Pistols were on the Today programme with the aforementioned Bill Grundy the whole fabric of society and who this small puffed up island belonged to culturally, almost physically shifted throughout the no more than three minute interview with these young crazy-looking spiky tops at the end of the programme. This sceptred isle, Blighty, strawberries and cream and tea on the lawn had just had a sudden stroke, one from which it never recovered.

That ridiculous speech John Major had made in the early 90s about spinsters on bicycles, warm beer and shadows getting longer on the cricket pitches was so out of step with the times because it had all been made redundant 15 years or so earlier by four young working class lads (the types at the time that were excluded from all things supposedly great and English) and their appearance on a teatime London news programme presented by the old hack Bill Grundy that seemed to hate the young counterculture that was, in their eyes, blighting Britain's perceived greatness. It was clearly a clash of culture made in heaven or hell, depending on which way you see it.

All it took was some badly chosen words from a drunk Steve

Jones, the Sex Pistols almost illiterate guitarist, a young bloke who before that had spent time in reform schools and borstals due to being a common thief, almost a Dickensian rapscallion, the type that was viewed with humour and laughable disdain from a society that looked on these people like they were Fagin's little boys in Oliver Twist's time; now here he was catapulting the faux stiff upper lipped England into the stratosphere and towards a dustbin far away.

If you've never seen the interview, the first thing to ask is where the hell have you been?! Also, how can you ever talk with knowledge about the demise or shifting sands of British society if you've no knowledge of the most important incident in post-war British cultural history.

Amazingly, Thames television originally had Queen booked to do the show, the band that had wooed the older record buyers and posh people after their smash hit single Bohemian Rhapsody with its classical interlude and Italian operetta pastiche that the pseudo intellectuals would have salivated over. This longer than usual 7-inch single, which in terms of running time came in at about seven minutes had spent some nine or 10 weeks at number one just a few months before. They had struck a chord with a certain chattering class section that tended not to like pop music made by what they probably saw as proles; however, Bohemian Rhapsody would have been in some cases the only record from the pop charts some plummy twats would have ever bought. Honestly, mate, Britain needed shaking up at the time!

This was going to be, I presume, some routine interview where they (Queen) would be very charming to the accommodating Grundy who liked classical music himself; however, call it fate, call it coincidence or an example of the chaos theory, or just a moment in history that happens to come along, they were to pull out at the last minute because allegedly Freddie Mercury had to go to the dentist! Rather than EMI just pull out altogether and there be no slot for a band to be on the show, or worse still Thames television ring one of their rivals at Polydor or A&M and get one of their hot young groups on, EMI and their record promoter, a man people may remember, Eric 'monster monster' Hall, persuaded the producer to put one of EMI's other acts The Sex Pistols on to the show instead. They were an up-and-coming group that represented the 'punk' movement in London that was happening at the time, although the chances of one of the suits in South Bank studios or indeed any big cheese at ITV knowing anything about this movement that was barely registering on the radar would be at best remote. Amazingly, they agreed though and Grundy, without much to go on in terms of research about the group, just ran with it and ran with it (I'm sure I can say without any fear of reprisals) half cut.

No doubt the Pistols were loaded as well, but what happened seemed to wrong foot Grundy and incredibly end his career that very afternoon!

At the beginning of the interview after a clip of the band playing, he says that they've received £40,000 from a record company and asked 'doesn't that seem opposed to the anti materialistic view of things?' – after not getting a satisfactory reply he says 'well tell me more then' to which the quite drunk Steve Jones says 'We've fucking spent it, ain't we'. He and the crew and director and everyone else completely missed that one. It went out live with no filter. A little later he (Grundy) goads John Lydon into swearing, to which John does and says shit, after the host gets him to repeat what he'd said before, then after Grundy tries to flirt with Siouxsie Sioux, with that Jones lets fly with a load of gleeful expletives. 'You dirty bastard', 'You dirty fucker', 'What a fucking rotter'. After this outburst, a clearly shaken Grundy who was doing his best to keep it all together looks down the camera and wraps up: 'Well that's it for tonight, the other rocker Eamonn I'm saying nothing about him, I'll be seeing you soon, hope I'm not seeing you again, from me though goodnight'. The signature tune 'Windy' plays out and history is made.

There was genuine shock after this happened. The headline the next day in the Daily Mirror is now an iconic one 'The Filth And The Fury' was the famous lead with I think an even better smaller headline afterwards 'TV Fury At Rock Cult Filth'. It was reported that one viewer was so mad that he kicked in the screen of his television set. Everything was now reset to ground zero, and all because of a suburban kid, a tea leaf from the Wormholt estate in Hammersmith swearing at an unlikeable journalist who thought he had these young upstarts in his back pocket. A previously unknown band became instantly infamous, the other half a dozen punk bands got immediate attention, and it's alleged that 300 groups were formed overnight to use Sex Pistols manager Malcolm Maclaren's words "from the wilds of Shropshire to Land's End".

It's hard to imagine how people could get so angry about words you hear routinely nowadays, but as someone who grew up in quite a rough small industrial town on Tyneside, swearing like that was confined to football matches, I presume work places, and kids at school when the teachers weren't about. There was no swearing in an official sense, certainly no toilet humour or mentioning of people's cycles or bodily functions. I remember hearing blokes apologise if they used bad language in front of women, and people told off for swearing on the bus or referring to anything in a graphic or pornographic sense. Also blaspheming was something that people didn't do. Even though church attendances had taken a real battering throughout the decade, people were reluctant to take the Lord's name in vain (I can't believe I'm even typing this!) in case someone wouldn't like it and pull them up for it. Casual racism was fine, but the bad language and the belittling of God and Jesus were off-limits.

At around this time and actually earlier than all this someone else was making a name for themselves with sweary, graphic tales and that was the Scottish comedian Billy Connolly. He had come to prominence on the folk music scene with Gerry Rafferty in The Humblebums, but now was solo and doing long stories in between the folk tunes and people were turning up for the funny routines rather than the folk music itself.

He was in part ridiculing the Catholic church and indeed the Christian faith in general with his five-minute monologues, the most famous one being about The Crucifixion where Jesus is portrayed as a Glasgow gang leader. Listening back to it, a young person would genuinely wonder what all the fuss was about, but because Britain and especially Scotland was a much more of a Christian society in those days, he was praised but scorned in equal measure. He was followed around outside the concert halls he was playing by Pastor Jack Glass, a protestant minister with his own church, very much a Scottish version of the Reverend Ian Paisley. Glass would stand outside the theatres and proclaim that Billy Connolly was a blasphemer and people shouldn't go and see him. This was real outrage and despite a lot of the younger, post-war baby boomer Scots celebrating this young man's work, much of Scotland couldn't in any way support this blasphemer. My own Scottish grandmother who was born in 1904 said to my father (her son) that this Billy Connolly was a 'terrible advert for Scotland'. As far as outrage goes, the likes of Connolly and later on The Sex Pistols were shaking up the noble image of the subservient working classes and pulling apart the romantic LS Lowry image of the working classes that were around before. Yes, the 60s Beat generation and with it the hippies and their free love were at odds with Britain and its colonial past, but now in the 1970s you had young people actually squaring up to the old way of life and doing that marvellous thing that the establishment hate, ie taking the piss out of it.

Right at the end of the decade the ultimate send-up of Christianity took place on the comedy front and that was Monty Python with their second film, The Life of Brian. Although Python had confused and baffled folk as well as entertained people at the same time, they never really courted controversy on a grand scale. I'm sure the film 'And Now for Something Completely Different', which was an amalgam of all of their celebrated sketches and the several wonderful TV series as well as the first proper film Monty Python And The Holy Grail got some people angry on different scales, but the first time they had a Lenny Bruce style gauntlet of hatred thrown at them was when they finally completed and released Brian.

To me outrage is a natural thing for much of the time. American heavy metal bands of the 80s with bandanas and tattoos putting their third fingers up at the camera on their photo shoots and declaring 'death to wimps' hasn't shocked anyone of note. The very people that are shocked by this would've been shocked by Andy Pandy and Emmerdale Farm, and to be honest wouldn't be the sorts of people that would subscribe to Kerrang magazine at that time, so the outrage serves no purpose whatsoever. Outrage and being just a bit tedious are two distinctly different things, yet some people can't really distinguish between the two.

Kenny Everett, the one-time loose cannon on British television and back in the 60s a real cult star on Radio Caroline, was involved with the Tory party and its campaigns in the 80s.

He claimed later that he "wasn't a full Tory" and that he only appeared at the 1983 Conservative Party Conference with his trademark foam hands from a preacher character he did on his BBC show because "the Tories had asked first". Whether this is to be believed or not is one thing, but what he said at the podium was surely meant to cause as much outrage as possible.

Before he went on stage, it was said by some that he should 'say something outrageous like let's bomb Russia', he explained that he couldn't say that as it was outrageous, but this was shouted down according to Kenny by film director Michael Winner who allegedly said "You're in the outrage business, darling".

'Let's bomb the Russians, yes let's kick Michael Foot's stick away' was hardly what you would call punching up but it did cause outrage at the time. Young people seem to think that there are those like Laurence Fox and Katie Hopkins now that say the most appalling things and that they're breaking new ground with this type of deliberately reprehensible behaviour, but it's taken place on a national scale since I'd say the Victorian era.

THE OUTRAGED

The outraged are always outraged. It's a permanent loop for them. There might be half a day when they're not outraged, but they're ironically comforted to know that something will come along for them to be outraged by before the end of the day.

At the time of writing this bit (October 2021) The PIF group with links to the Saudi Government have taken over the football club Newcastle United in an estimated 300-million-pound deal. Allegedly they paid a billion pounds to BEIN Sports based in the UAE over pirate infringements to smooth out a deal without BEIN or the English FA getting in the way. They plan to spend a lot of money and this has instantly made a provincial football club the richest in the world. Amongst the inevitable observations that this is now the death of competition and that money is ruining the game, there has been a political debate about human rights abuses in Saudi Arabia and that the Public Investment Fund buying a well-known football club with almost 130 years of history is merely 'sportswashing', and if Newcastle United fans had anything about them at all they'd demonstrate, march, stop buying merchandise or better still refuse to go and watch their football club at all just because of the mere shame of them being linked with all this murder, persecution and genocide. Of course, this to a small extent is a legitimate argument, but the outpouring of outrage was as big LAST week as it is SMALL this week. Yes, it was a week ago but the 'outraged' are getting ready to be aghast at something else coming this week, so the fury toward the Middle East consortium has quelled. It's like the House of Saud can crack on now because the outrage rather like a heavy wind has passed.

A few years ago, people were outraged about 'poverty porn' due to documentaries like Channel 4's Benefit Street in 2014. People were almost taking to the streets because it apparently showed benefit claimants in what they thought the programme makers were trying to imply 'their real light', ie claiming and thus receiving all kinds of benefits but living a life of relative luxury on a sink estate, drinking and taking drugs every day and having all the mod cons but not actually working for a living. Like a lot of Channel 4 programmes from the day the channel started back in 1982, it's tried to put the cat amongst the pigeons and light the blue touch paper as far as viewer feedback goes. People were outraged, then a week later...people weren't.

Boris Johnson's perceived racism, people trafficking, MPs' expenses, Harvey Weinstein, Bill Cosby, the Orange Order, people's salaries at the BBC, the lack of women on panel shows, people from the Windrush generation being deported, and on and on it goes; for a length of time the outraged are outraged, then there's this oasis of calm till the next one hits. Next week's fish and chip paper was the old fashioned phrase; last week's outraged tweets is probably more apt for the 21st century.

THE IGNORANCE OF MONEY AND THE PERCEPTION OF WEALTH

EARNING MONEY

'Say what you like about Adolf Hitler but I wouldn't have minded his money'. That was a joke of mine that never worked. It has been hidden in other routines and carried along as a pastiche of how people speak but it's never been a standalone joke that weekend audiences have liked. Comics like it, well at least they've told me that they do, and it works in company and amongst hip late-night crowds at the Edinburgh Fringe or somewhere like that, but it's probably being clever for clever's sake and will always lose out to the previous act on stage saying 'I've been married for 20 years now, you only get 15 for murder'.

My joke is about how British people look at someone and however reprehensible that person's actions were, they've done well financially so they can't be all bad. I got lectured about money throughout my early working life. 'The election will be won and lost on tax' was always a line trotted out by the old twats at work who fancied themselves as intellectual heavyweights. As young people, money and what other people's salary was, was never a driving force for many of us. I could be wrong here, but from about my generation onwards it was all about liking a job and getting job satisfaction and loving coming into work, rather than spitting tacks because someone elsewhere doing an even more mundane job than you was getting £750 a year more and getting a company car so by rat race logic they were doing better – ah bloody hell I must find that soul destroying job that pays more in order to make it look like I'm winning in life.

Nowadays people strive to enjoy their working life and that's the top priority over money and surely that's how it should be considering you're a long time dead, isn't it? As long as you don't starve I'd prefer to look forward to my Monday mornings rather than count off the days till retirement and death.

However, money and what sort of money people earn has been fertile ground for people talking out of their arse for years. Here's my favourite. 'So, say you were on about £15 a week back in the 1960s and say you're on £350 now, right then how much is a pint? Well if you work that out, you were better off then when you think about it.' Ah it's so correct yet so wrong at the same time, isn't it. What a classic example of seeing the world through the eyes of a white working class male weekend drinker! The price of a pint symbolising how people were better off in the halcyon 1960s as that's the barometer of pleasure, enlightenment and aspiration amongst all of society. What about the people who don't drink? What about people who liked fancy drinks like gin and orange, or vodka and Tia Maria, or people who did all their drinking in the house? Or were they saying that a pint represented the price of pretty much everything back in the day and is linked with all aspects of day-to-day living then and of course is directly proportional with multicultural box-set Britain today? I suspect, like I suspect throughout this book, that they haven't a fucking clue what they're talking about. Pints of bitter and lager and half a light ale? It's a frivolity, isn't it? It's not groceries to keep you and your family alive. The pictures? Bloody hell, man, even in the supposedly hungry 1930s there's stories aplenty about people going to the pictures, taking their future husband or wife when they were courting and getting all misty eyed about the adverts in the cinemas, the usherettes, the sweeties and the cost in the circle being more or less than the stalls and you could get two in the gods and get a choc bar and get the bus there and back and still have change from an arbitrary amount of money etc. To be honest, I always stopped listening after a few minutes. Remember apparently how cheap it was to get into the Palais or the greyhounds and how there were loads of snooker halls? If you're of my generation and a bit younger, you would've been overloaded with tales from grandparents and old uncles and aunties telling you about such things and it then makes you think that the middle of the 20th century wasn't as austere as they like to make you think. I don't know of any British people of Middle Eastern descent saying that they're much worse off because the price of baklava has increased significantly compared to wages in the olden days, yet the white working classes do this all the time and try and prove some sort of vague point and it of course sits perfectly with the Napoleon idea that we're all shopkeepers counting the coppers and using that as a litmus test as to how much of a good time we're having.

As a side note and probably the answer to this 'pints' question, I'm afraid beer back in the 70s in the main was pretty bloody awful. I'm sorry that this bit is subjective rather than objective, but you can't compere craft beers now that are made with care and perfection and TLC with piss like Norseman Lager, Harp and Watney's Red Barrel. Yes, it's all about personal taste, but I think if there was an actual taste test, the independent brewers of today that you pay a bit of a premium for would win with a North Korean landslide and it wouldn't even be rigged over the hard water hogwash that was drunk in Pontins, working men's clubs and the Dog and Fungus on the High Street.

Of course, the answer isn't to do with pounds and pence, it's cultural, isn't it. Don Revie, the late former England football manager and infamous boss of Leeds United before that, who transformed a nonentity of a football club in a very famous north of England city into a sporting phenomenon, divided opinion even 30 years after his untimely death to motor neurone disease in 1989. He was a bloke who allegedly took bungs and bribes and offered them out to others at a regular rate. 'Don Readies' they used to call him. It's well known that Leeds United were hated not just for the fact that they kicked other teams upside down, but that they allegedly leaned on refs and tried to nobble the authorities. It was a period of English football that, looking back, was a terrific time to be a football fan because of the intrigue and the pantomime revulsion of these johnny-come-lately bandits like Leeds United ruining our lovely game and stopping it from being this noble Roy Of The Rovers type boys comic bob hat and rattle pastime, and putting it straight into the dirty, grimy muck and brass 'Play For Today' adults-only game that oversaw football's peak in my view in the 1970s. Revie's Leeds were the main team, they were box office. Apparently, opposition managers were approached and offered money on a regular basis to lie down and let Revie's team win.

Anyway, in 1962 at around Easter time, Revie approached another manager, Bob Stokoe, just before a game for Leeds away to Bury (Stokoe was the Bury manager at the time) and offered him £500 if his lads 'took it easy today'. Apparently Stokoe said 'not bloody likely' then went into the director's office and told his chairman who in turn told him to keep it quiet. The revelations never came out till about 15 years later when Stokoe told this story to a journalist and allegedly broke down in tears while telling it. It was around the time that Revie's former goalkeeper Gary Sprake had claimed to the press that Revie had been bribing rival clubs left, right and centre and was involved in throwing matches for the last couple of decades during Sprake's time at the club.

My point to all this is that those previous people mentioned, the bar room arse talkers, would say 'well how much was a pint? I'd reckon all Stokoe could have got out of £500 in those days was about 2,000 pints which isn't a fortune he'd have drunk that in a couple of years, yes a classic tale of the innocent post-war era ebbing away and being replaced for the brave new world of the 1960s, the white heat of technology on the one hand as Harold Wilson so boldly put it, but with Profumogate and other such scandals coming out, the jolly hockey stick 1950s were giving way to a stark exposé of seedy deals and dirty skulduggery that was rapidly putting to an end the Victorian valued Ovaltine Britain and sweeping in this sinister era that was to gain traction throughout the years after...but being explained in monetary terms by twats in pubs about amounts of pints!

In all seriousness, £500 in 1962 is worth (according to a calculator app) £7458.49 in today's money, but it's not really, is it, it's a lot more than that when you look at it culturally. Commentators on the right think that working class people's living standards are going up every year, but it's all relative, and they make this common mistake of thinking that advancing living standards and changes in technology are one and the same. Just because you can watch Game of Thrones on widescreen in your own living room doesn't mean that your mortality rate just got better. It's apples and oranges, and once again it's people judging morality exactly the same from one era to another, despite them being nearly 60 years apart. In 1962 I bet that most working class people had never even seen £500 or knew anyone with that sort of money, let alone have it themselves, it's a mental amount of money because of the freedom it would've afforded you, especially getting it all in one go in an envelope. It's an amount of money that if invested wisely would've seen you open a business with a 90% chance of untold riches. It's not like getting seven and a half grand today that might just ease your credit card debt: £500 in 1962 would've got you a house albeit a fairly modest 2 bedroom terraced house up north but the alleged incident took place up north so it counts.

No one went on gap years in 1962, no blokes went on male maternity leave or did their coal mining job from home to look after the kids while their wife went back to her career. Nobody in 1962 just went part-time at the shipyard so they could write a book, and there were no instances in 1962 where people that had been made redundant in the foundry weren't hurrying back to work because they were going to just play golf for a while because their DFT shares were doing really well because of a strong Hang Seng. People didn't get left 50 grand by their Auntie Maureen — yes, people did come into money but it was such a rare thing compared to today and it was just modest amounts left by people who put a few quid aside in the post office. Also, you either wrote out cheques because your money was in the bank, or you paid for stuff with cash. There was no credit as such, certainly not for the working people, and working till you dropped down dead was paradoxically a way of life. People got stuff on the never-never (my grandmother worked as a money lender and people just didn't pay her) and couldn't pay it off. The problems people had were similar to today's problems, but

£500 cash would change all that in an instant and having enough pints wouldn't be one of the pitfalls.

Employers these days aren't stupid, and the consumer world has got people by the genitals. If an employer was to say "I'd really like to poach you from that place you work now and you come and work for my company, but I appreciate that it'll be hard to get you to come across so how about first I pay off your mortgage and all your credit card debts so you've nothing to worry about? Obviously your salary will be low after that but you'd be much happier and have lots of financial security" – that would sound great, wouldn't it? The thing is no employer is ever going to say or do that, are they, they don't want someone who is in the comfort zone, someone who knows that if things start to slide it doesn't really matter, someone who isn't hungry to get on or a person on a mission, it's easy street and everyone knows it. These days, of course, people are on zero hours contracts, we've got a minimum wage but what bloody use is that if you don't know whether you'll still be in a job next week? Also, the minimum wage is pretty poor anyway, so we've lost out in all ways. In my view, if you're working and even if you're working in a good job, you're kept but you're just kept enough to keep you onside. If you're paid shite money with no hope whatsoever of being comfortable for the rest of your working life, you'll have nowt to lose and the last thing any government wants is their citizens with nowt to lose. On the other side of the coin, you can't have a country where everyone is fairly comfortable because there's a worry that they'll tell the daft baldy bastard that runs the firm to fuck off. There's a worry that people will say 'Oh I don't need this shit' and walk away and do something rewarding for a fraction of the money, you know heaven forbid something they enjoy, but once again we're brought down to Earth by the salary debate from people trotting out lines from the popular press. 'So if Labour get in you'd pay a load more tax, you'd be happy with that, would you, paying a load more tax, would you, eh?'… 'yes'… 'Ah right you'd be happy paying more tax than you are now, would you?'… 'yes'… 'Ah yes, very clever saying yes when you mean no.'

A widescreen telly with the latest HD, an American style fridge or no more mortgage payments again? I know which one I would choose, but we're told that the latest thing is what we want! Anyway, if you had no more mortgage payments to pay you could easily save up for a huge telly or a massive fridge in a matter of weeks, no plastic involved whatsoever.

As I say, and I've said this from the start, you're quite welcome to disagree with many of the things I say in this book and many of my observations, but after a half a century on this planet and someone who engages people for a living, I'd say we're all sold a lifestyle lie. I'm not the first commentator to say that we don't need the mod cons, there's been legions before me, but I'd just like to say I'm the latest one to say it and we're not wrong.

BIG BUSINESS

'BIG BUSINESS IS VERY WISE, CROSSING OVER INTO
ENTERPRISE' – JOHN LYDON 1983

I remember a young chap working in a hotel I was staying in, who came out with this affected, atypical nonsense that we always hear about when it comes to perceived big business and entrepreneurs. Just to set the scene, it was the Holiday Inn in Dartford on University Way, just next to the M25 and a couple of goal kicks away from the Dartford crossing, that great feat of engineering which has now turned into a belter of a hidden tax machine from the Blairite dynasty that shapes the sort of 'you'll be forced to pay for any piece of shit we're offering' society we find ourselves in now. It was sort of fitting that he should come out with this balls when we were in the shadow of this money making monster. We were at the bar, I was having a late drink after work and he was serving, and there was a political debate programme going on on the television a few feet in front of us. He turned to me and said, "You know, why do we let politicians run this country? We've got great businessmen and they're really good at making business work and making profits, why don't they run the place instead of these politicians who know nothing about business." Yes, the cliché klaxons were sounding off in all chambers of my head upon hearing this! I gave him the most articulate and sane answer I could without getting patronising and I used as much humility as I could so as not to look like 'Norman Know All', but bloody hell it's difficult, isn't it, to keep one's head when people (and I bet he's not the only one) spout utter shite like this in front of you.

What is it in this country and the cult of 'big business'??? What is it with worshipping the Dragon's Den people and Alan Sugar as well as Richard Branson and Mike Ashley, Philip Green and the woman who founded The Body Shop? This American dream that Amazon and Disney started life in a garage and that most businesses started off small? What a bombshell to find out that they were small businesses first and then they grew?!! Mind blowing, isn't it!

Anyway, where do you start. First of all, Alan Sugar, Mike Ashley. Are those people successful? Honestly, are they? Sugar has been responsible for stuff that has had dreadful reviews over the years. Do I need a citation for this? Not really. The Amstrad TS88 Hi-fi system, the Amstrad computers and word processors, the Amstrad fax machines. I don't need to say anymore, do I? I don't need to say anything libellous, slanderous or defamatory, I just need to say look at the reviews of those products and then tell me what I've said wrong. Actually, I'll give you some anecdotal evidence. I had an Amstrad TS88 as a present from my parents I think for my 14th birthday in 1983; the thing broke just after the warranty ran out (a common problem with the cassettes where you could record from one cassette to the other and there was a problem with the mechanism jamming). It was intimated that Amstrad designed them to work for about a year before they went wrong, by which time the year's warranty was over and they weren't obliged to fix it for free. What happened with those products wasn't what you'd call successful, but if you wanted to say that it brought in a lot of money for Mr Sugar you'd be correct, I think, in that assumption. I'd like to think that Mr Sugar made a lot of money for himself out of these electrical products, but is that success? Does it employ people en masse that would have been employed anyway? Does it make for a fairer Britain? Did these products get sold around the world? If they did, was it of his doing, or a marketing team working for him to earn him more money and them bonuses? For the record I've never heard of a TS88 in a house somewhere abroad, maybe I've not looked hard enough or spoken to the right people in the many countries I've visited.

An entrepreneur, especially a billionaire one, doesn't create wealth, it doesn't trickle down; they keep it for themselves. Nothing wrong with that in my view, I'm not a communist, but these people that get other people to make shite stuff for them for low amounts of money in order to make themselves very rich have, in some people's opinion, to be given the opportunity to solve the UK's strained transport network despite all the intricate problems that go with it, or get the keys to the NHS yearly windfall so they can make it work better.

Harold Wilson, love him or hate him, wanted to be the world's greatest statistician, he was one of the youngest Oxford dons aged 21 and was a lecturer in Economic history at New College Oxford; Margaret Thatcher had two degrees, one in law where she specialised in taxation and the other a BSc in Chemistry, like Wilson at Oxford. Also, she worked at Lyons perfecting emulsifiers for ice cream which was ground-breaking at the time. Aye, that's right, let's fuck this lot off for people who sold cheap Donnay socks and golf umbrellas at their chain of Sports shops alongside Mr Mouthpiece who flogged computers that invariably lost data.

'The state?! It couldn't run a chip shop' said some old goat in the House of Lords once when I was half watching it on telly about 30 years ago. He sounded like a captain of industry with his sort of soft cockney accent. I bet the silly old twat was rehearsing that all night beforehand knowing that, ironically enough, a load of dole wallers would be watching him live the next afternoon on BBC2. Also, it's another silly, cliched soundbite to appease the hard of thinking once again. Who's to say a chip shop isn't hard to run?! I can imagine a lot of people have tried to run a successful chip shop over the years, but due to I don't know it being in the wrong place geographically, ie far too near a couple of very successful chippies, using bad suppliers, not being a skilled fish fryer, prices too high/too low, bad customer service, a bad food hygiene rating due to lack of cleanliness, maybe being too fastidious so they take too long to serve people, and any number of other things, it's failed and closed its doors; it might be Alan and his wife Beryl, but they're still the private sector and they've still failed at something that apparently is so easy, the state could come close to running.

Also, the very people that would think that that phrase was terrific are the sorts of aforementioned people like the Dartford barman that would salivate over the idea of the head of Harry Ramsdens becoming minister of fucking education in his utopian British future.

Just when the first lockdown was winding down and people became a little less anxious about catching the virus, the shops opened — or should I say, the non-essential shops. It was 15th June 2020. The Sun newspaper, that bastion of consumerism and housewife's choice articles, the paper that has sub columns like 'When To Do The Ironing' for a programme that they don't rate, said that it was your 'civic responsibility' to go to the shops on opening day and spend some money to stimulate the economy. Now I really don't want to know how many people live their lives around The Sun's editorial 'The Sun Says' but it's a bit like finding out the actual amount of people that died horrific deaths during the Chernobyl disaster, I'd be really upset if I knew the actual number but I don't doubt it's a canny few. People piling into

Primark en masse and stuffing their trolley full of shit was sometimes more depressing to look at than nurses struggling on Covid wards a few weeks before. The idea of it being some sort of civic duty to spend money on stuff you literally didn't need brought it home that this oasis of calm from mid-March to mid-June was exactly just that, an oasis that we'd soon be out of, and people then would be reverting to type and keeping these big companies going with their very small amounts of disposable income.

I don't want to go all 'lefty' as the right wingers might say and proclaim that it's the government's responsibility to give money out and stimulate the economy and handouts will save the world etc (that was a bit crass but you get the idea), but the general dictum that people have to spend money on stuff that is at best titilatory to help us get out of financial hardship is a slap in the face to people who socially distanced, were really thorough with handwashing, went without seeing their nearest and dearest for months and watched every turgid news conference on the BBC at 5 o'clock every night. Mr Primark's in trouble and he needs your help is sort of Lord Kitchener speak for the 21st century consumer age, and people went shopping straight away partly for stuff because they'd missed shopping for stuff and partly to save Britain if the Sun was to be believed.

To be fair, if there was no Primark (by the way other chain stores are available) there'd be something else in its place and I'm sure the masses would have piled into there on June

15th instead. The thing I'm arguing is this: do people really need stuff? Again, don't think that I've gone all brothers of the soil commune on you; I like things, I like gadgets, quirky stuff for the house, some decent good looking jeans, a nice polo shirt and lovely tiles for the shower and stuff for the garden, as well as little pictures that are a conversation piece when people come round, I'm a slave to shite just the same as you are, but I went weeks through lockdown with some socks and underpants and because I had time to wash them and in the case of the socks pair them!!, I found myself collecting the socks and underpants from the beginning of the week from the washer, putting them back in the drawer all clean and fresh and thus the drawers were busting full of a veritable underpant and sock overload that I previously had no idea about. Basically, the little presents from the missus to keep me going, ie an underpants three-pack or a set of socks, some sports socks for 5-a-side, birthday underpants, Christmas socks, Father's Day comfy socks, special treat long legged underpants and of course me on the road saying to myself that actually I need a couple of pairs of underpants. I didn't!! And I continue to not need them now. I can wash the bastards and as long as I keep a bit of order on the washing, drying and ironing like I'm running a small factory, I probably need never get a pair of Tommy Hilfigers again. I have enough underclothes; that part of the economy can go on something else.

SMALL BUSINESS

Back in the 80s, I remember Geordie blokes saying to me 'my mate's a barber and he says he'll be alright because everyone's ganna need a haircut like'. That one didn't really work out, did it?!! It turns out that a number 1, 2 or 3 haircut can be done to a competent level with your own affordable trimming tools and this has been the case for some time now. I'd say that the 'Salon' may well be thriving where a lot of women (and blokes) like to see their own hair as a passion or a project, and like painting the Forth Bridge, or rather maintaining the Sistine Chapel ceiling, such is their attention to detail to roots, dead ends and the overall finished masterpiece of the hair they feel that it's a never ending job and always needing to be improved to suit their weight, their mood and the changing trends in the world of self-image. Why not though?! If that's your thing good on you, and as a by-product if these salon moguls get rich then c'est la vie! Good on them and good on you for making your hair look nice; it makes, I think, for a better world.

A lot of blokes now shave off all of their hair rather than do the classic Bobby Charlton combover that was big for a long time right up until the late 80s when actor Gregor Fisher, famous for his portrayal of Scottish working class philosopher Rab C Nesbitt, had another character called 'The Baldy Man' who had a big combover. This character wasn't really very celebrated or taken to by the general public when his character was in his own sitcom of the same name; however, the Baldy Man was on an advert for Hamlet cigars, a long running advert that involved lots of different people in different scenarios where something unfortunate, usually involving a bit of slapstick, would happen to the protagonist in the advert and they'd then reach to their pocket for a Hamlet which they'd light up and a bit of melancholy Bach started playing and the narrator would say 'happiness is a cigar called Hamlet, the mild cigar'. To the young people, I'm not making this shit up, this was believe it or not, a way of selling consumer goods to people back in our youth!! Anyway, for the Baldy Man Hamlet ad, he was in a photo booth getting some photos done to make him look still quite the catch despite the combover. He was just getting the hair swept across his head to create the illusion of having a full head of hair, then all of a sudden the adjustable seat gave way and the camera flashed. He then lit up and the narrator kicked in.

A barber was telling me once that loads of blokes at the time of that advert came into the barbers and said, I saw that advert and thought 'bloody hell who am I trying to kid' and then said 'just cut it all off'. To me it proves that any kind of clever gameplay or supposedly inspiring marketing can be rendered useless by something innocent like that. When someone invests in something and tells you those immortal words 'this is the future' it more often than not tends not to be.

Similarly...

NO ONE IS DOING THIS ANYMORE

I've always been wary of the whole 'you might as well switch over because no one else is doing this anymore' mantra. Are people trying to shame you into changing your allegiance to the latest thing? Are they telling you for your own good so you don't make a fool of yourself/get ripped off/have to completely re-train in the future in front of someone else? Who knows but the phrase crops up an awful lot.

Back in early 1987 I briefly had a factory job in a Press shop. It was one of many factory jobs I had, but this one was, believe it or not, even more boring than all of the other factory jobs that I had. Basically, presses are machines that have a tool that pounces down on a raw material and presses them into shape. They're used in the car industry a lot. Light metals (aluminium, mild steel, tin etc) can be made into a user-friendly shape very quickly, especially when a machine with great force is transferring rotary motion into linear motion by the means of a tool slide at a repetitive rate onto said material. Anyway, it was bloody stultifying watching the machine all day knock out a million components at a time and I had to check the odd one to see that they were still running okay. There's only so much I could do, but I had to look busy otherwise I would get wrong.

My boss was a classic wanker, he even had a wanker's voice. It was squeaky like a dog's toy and he talked a fuck of a lot. He was from South-West London which was quite rare in the North-East in those days, but he sounded like a grass on the Sweeney and even though it was ten years later dressed like that sort of idiot as well with kipper ties and massive collars and flares. You know the type 'alright Reagan, I'll give you a couple of names if you let me walk'. Anyway he 'knew' everything, he was a perfect case study for this book. When he wasn't telling me how clever his kids were and telling me that my work wasn't even as good as his kids' hypothetical day's work that day should they be able to reach the machines, and telling me that he was once in a band and they were brilliant but they had to pack in because they were making too much money (you get the idea of the sort of 24 carat prick we're talking about), he was always telling me about the future of engineering, commerce and Britain, as well as his firm and how well that was going (he got his business wound up not long after I left the place), no subject was off the table as to how much he knew about it and he'd chuckle at our lack of knowledge of said topic.

One of the things he was interested in was not liking sport.

It's weird, isn't it, it's a bit like obsessive atheism, people spend their lives telling other people how rubbish something is that they personally don't like and it seems that they're draining so much energy out of themselves by physically hating it so much that you begin to feel sorry for their hating obsession! There he was though every Monday morning:

'So what did you do on Saturday?'

'Watched Newcastle play.'

'No doubt they got hammered.'

'No, they won.'

'Who were they playing, the blind school?!'

This conversation happened week after week, regardless of the score at the weekend. Do you know what, I'm going to throw it out there and say that I don't think he was actually listening to the answer before reaching for his trusty blind school punchline and he chuckled to himself like it was the first time he said it and that he had us on the ropes with his rapier wit. I always felt like just one Monday saying 'Of course they weren't playing the blind school, you ignorant cunt, do you really think that the blind school are in the English First Division? They were playing Aston Villa as it happened, another team of non-blind players that are grown men partaking in a sport where you have to be very fit and talented to play professionally, oh and by the way it's 1987, the whole blind school thing is on its way out, someone with limited, blurred or complete sight loss nowadays just goes to mainstream school because outside of that one limitation in life they're just like me and you, well maybe not you, you fucking social retard'. Anyway I didn't say that, I would probably have been sacked, so I just went along with him 'ah blind school ha ha' and he would go about his day thinking that he was the Oscar Wilde of the industrial unit.

One of his kids was interested in American football or whatever it was called then. I'm not a fan myself (but do you know what? If it's on the telly I just change the channel to something I like, crazy isn't it), so I wasn't getting the names of the teams right – once again he was throwing his head back and laughing at my lack of knowledge and he said that there was loads of people at some local game somewhere in Prudhoe or Stocksfield or one of them small towns in the Northumbrian Tyne Valley near where he lived, then followed it up with "No one wants to watch football any more". On another occasion a few weeks later, I remember another employee said that the 100th anniversary of the Football League commemorative game at Wembley was only two thirds full to which right on cue he said, "I've told ya, no one wants to watch football anymore, people find it boring".

I'd love to find him now, whether he's got another press tool company or whether he branched out and gone into business somewhere working in one of the other fields that he knows loads about and had foresight and can see what's coming over the hill, like the demise of the national game. No doubt he's probably retired and having to rely heavily on a state pension judging by the two businesses he oversaw going down the pan in the late 80s. To these types of people though, getting stuff all wrong or actually predicting something and the actual polar opposite happening is just water off a duck's back. I bet they don't even remember making these wild claims, they'll be boring people to death right now about how no one wants this anymore or no one wants that anymore, and then in the future when you want to find them to gleefully tell them that they got it spectacularly wrong, they've disappeared and they're on to the next victim with their vacuous points based on no knowledge or collated evidence.

I've another lovely example from another Londoner, but this one was many years later and in a totally different industry altogether. It was about the turn of the millennium and I had been given a free place (paid for by the BBC or Northern Arts or some bloody quango that the creative types don't seem to fully appreciate as free shit that other people don't get) to go on a course in Newcastle for a couple of days about comedy and comedy writing and what sort of stuff they were looking for today so you could become the next big comedy writer from the patronised provinces. It was on over two days and all the people who were tenuously linked to comedy in the Tyne and Wear area were packed into this room to listen to expert advice. Once again, this was a lovely example of the people I've based this book on!

Anyway, this bloke turned up from Channel 5 and told us all about what was in and what was out in the world of comedy commissioning and what the do's and don'ts were involving writing to try and get a commission, also what the gatekeepers in television these days were like and what their mindset was in terms of what they were seeing as the future of TV comedy. Believe me, every postmodern comedian has been to something like this in their time, because I've been around for 28 years and been seen as 'promising new talent' for a good chunk of that, they think the best way to move you on or shut you up is for you to listen to a posh man for an hour tell you how hard it is to get anything made but send stuff through anyway.

Sadly I can't remember his name, but he informed us that he absolutely loved the city and used to live at Two Ball Lonnen, a rough suburb in the west end of Newcastle, when he worked as a researcher on The Tube in the early 80s (The Tube was a youth TV programme on Channel 4 that was quite revolutionary at the time and still held a lot of kudos because of its alternative live bands and lots of chaos in between; this was obviously a way of getting a few brownie points with the 'hip' gathering in the room) and he was so pleased to be back. We were in a building right next to the railway station – no doubt as soon as he was done he was out of there like jack fucking flash and straight on to the next Inter City to King's Cross!

Who am I to be cynical though as he was taking his time to

tell us all about the industry and his big thing all the way through the talk was that sitcoms are on the way out. No need to write an old fashioned sitcom because there'll be no more of those things made in future and he was very confident in that assumption. The reason for this — and I've never forgotten this line and it's something that cheers me up when I'm down — was that 'no one talks like that anymore'!! Ah joy! Yes, he really fucking well said that. Ah man, where do you start?! The idea that people spoke like Frank Spencer back in 1974 is risible in the extreme. He was a funny character with a silly voice that went in for slapstick, it wasn't Play For Today! I really don't remember people in the near past having the ready wit of someone like Basil Fawlty, otherwise he wouldn't have been running a crappy Torquay hotel, rather he would've been a wonderful television writer and hailed as the greatest quickfire satirist of all time alongside Oscar Wilde, WC Fields or Mark Twain, such was his intellectual dexterity to pull out an apt phrase for the immediate situation he was in, however difficult it was. Imagine a set of real-life characters like the ones in The Fall and Rise of Reginald Perrin or a bunch of cartoon set up punchline one liner merchants in a real South London pub like in Only Fools And Horses. I guarantee a real life Wolfie Smith wouldn't have been crash bang wallop funny like Robert Lindsay was who portrayed him, or have a semi daft bespectacled mate called Ken and another pal who had a penchant for country music and dressing like a cowboy, it was a bit of fun as a sitcom is supposed to be. Caricatures with gag heavy lines and ludicrous storylines to make you piss yourself laughing, that's what it was AND STILL IS!

He was obsessed with the 'two camera' comedy like The Office and The Royle Family because that's the way comedy was apparently now headed, a sort of real life type of route and a window into that real life and of course 'no one wants to watch traditional sitcoms any more' because 'no one talks like that anymore'.

Once again, I'd love to bump into him now, I bet he's still stealing a living somewhere in television, probably doing that those that can't do teach type of roles for some group of people willing to part money for his 'expertise and experience'. He's probably, as you're reading this right now, telling some group of young hopefuls that the way forward is to actually write a sitcom like Miranda, Mrs Brown's Boys or Not Going Out, as they're great examples of humour to get away from these boring two camera comedies that end up looking like kitchen sink plays rather than funny shows. I'm sure he'll be out the door as soon as his time's up ready to dash back to the railway station for the last commuter train back to London and looking forward to the BACS payment a few days later.

I suppose I've used a lot of anecdotal evidence quite a bit, but here's a couple more to hang your hat on. Remember when retail experts said that there was no use for vinyl anymore and that CDs were the way forward? Yes, that was a classic custard pie moment for the music experts, and on the subject of the music industry of course the most famous conversation in pop music history of course was thus "Guitar groups are on the way out, Mr Epstein". Dick Rowe of Decca went to his grave in 1986 denying that he'd ever said this to Brian Epstein, the then Beatles manager; well of course he would, wouldn't he! No one is going to admit to being that big a chump. Dick Rowe of Decca famously knocked The Beatles back and it was claimed in Brian Epstein's autobiography that the full statement was "Not to mince words, Mr Epstein, we don't like your boys' sound. Groups of guitars are on the way out ... Your boys are never going to get off the ground. We know what we're talking about. You really should stick to selling recordings in Liverpool." (From: Brian Epstein, A Cellarful of Noise London: Souvenir, 1964).

In Rowe's defence he did sign The Rolling Stones, Them (with Van Morrison), Lulu, Tom Jones, The Animals, The Moody Blues, The Zombies and The Small Faces amongst others, but when one looks at those signings, the majority tend to be guitar bands as if Mr Rowe was overcompensating for the fact that he'd dropped a huge bollock with The Beatles. It is rumoured that several years later, probably at the dying end of the 1960s, a very young David Bowie and Marc Bolan were in his waiting room and he yelled at his secretary 'Get these hippies out of my office and find me the new Beatles'. It's probably apocryphal, but it's a funny little tale all the same. The ironic thing for me is that when it comes to the Simon Cowells of this world who seems to be some sort of Judge Dredd 'my word is law' in the music industry, a Dick Rowe in my opinion is exactly what we need at the moment. Someone to get something spectacularly wrong and then be exposed for it. Something to prove to us that the game of entertainment isn't rigged and that the big boys as well as the little people punching up can get things all wrong at times.

Going back to Brian Epstein though and stories from the past almost frozen in time can prove the naivety of the era and that's fair enough, but once again people with no grasp of the past, the future and the present for that matter often ridicule it in turn but not apply any logic or understanding of the fact that it was in the past. Apparently, in the early days of The Beatles, Epstein had their unique Beatles logo with the drop T designed for him by a feller called Ivor Arbiter who owned a drum shop where Ringo had recently acquired a brand new drum kit and it was painted on the drums by a local signwriter called Eddie Stokes. It is said that the drum shop was paid five pounds for the design! This unique and what was to become iconic logo was something that Epstein realised could earn him some easy money and not long after that was meeting with business people I presume in the patent side of the industry. What is chronicled at the time was that Epstein was very proud of a deal he'd negotiated whereby he was to get 10% of everything that people manufactured and retailed with The Beatles logo on it. It no doubt looked like a great deal at the time because the money would just roll in and as anyone would tell you in the performing, intellectual and artistic rights game, you can earn as you sleep. It's clear now that he should have been getting 90% rather than 10%, as that's the sort of figure you'd get now, but in the documentaries I've heard the general consensus is that Epstein was a bloody idiot and was hoodwinked by these much more switched on blokes in the room. The fact was no one had ever negotiated this kind of deal before, and it was breaking new ground. Once again 1963 isn't 2020 and no one, least of all people that went to work for a living, would have known that he was at the wrong end of the scale when it's clear he was in the driving seat and could have driven a hard bargain for what was the youth sensation of the country and soon to be the world.

This was all in the distant past and the benefit of hindsight keeps these empty vessels that comment on such innocent aspects of recent history smug and self-aggrandising. Of course, no one negotiates crap deals for popular music bands anymore, but if Epstein hadn't negotiated that one in the first place who knows where we would be in the evolution of getting paid a retainer if the name of your band in a certain type of font is emblazoned on merchandise. Yes, the people sneering without context would have done so much better if they'd had some sort of time machine; however, invariably where the self-titled business minded know-alls get found out is when they predict the future...

IT'S JUST BUSINESS

It's just business say people who've never run a business. What people who've never run a business never get is the fact that you can't just tell people to 'fuck off' if they deliver things late/provide a shoddy service/overcharge for something that could've been a lot cheaper. You can be a bit pissed off and you can make your feelings known, but expletives and threatening to break legs aren't a good look. The thing is, you have to work with people. Even if it's a temporary arrangement you learn to do business with people courteously or you'd get a reputation of being a massive wanker yourself, even if you feel that you're the righteous one. These people that say 'eeeh I'd be terrible me I wouldn't stand for any kind of shit' are the sorts that would have to wind their businesses up after a year because they'd managed to piss off the few precious customers they'd initially got. I've had people tell me this week that they've now put on their invoices that people must pay within 30 days and (their words) 'if it goes to 31 they get a CCJ'. This is the sort of thing you can do for a little while but (and sorry if this sounds obvious to people in business) it would go around very quickly that you were a difficult bastard and people that sometimes pay in 30 days but sometimes it drags on a couple of weeks will not work for you at all and link themselves with someone else that isn't going to take them to court at the drop of a hat.

THIS IS THE FUTURE

'Believe you me, this is the future'. I've heard all that from digital recording and floppy discs to CNC production and Fortran computer language. A bloke I worked with in a call centre would talk lots about the future and what was in store, he was that classic, 'no one does this anymore' and 'this is the way forward'. I can't remember his name, it might have been Steve, and although he was a bit patronising and flash and looked about 10 years out of date in the mid-90s, he wasn't too bad a bloke, so with that I was prepared to put up with his self-congratulatory alleged pearls of wisdom. Anyway, he left the company to start up his own business developing people's photographs, you know from people's 30 mm cameras onto film. This is in about 1997 he started a photo development company. I mean, you don't need me to extrapolate into words the way that that business went by virtue of some sort of graph, do you???

RELIGION
AND
POLITICS

RELIGION AND ANTI-RELIGION

'It's 2019, folks, we don't need religion.' I've always shaken my head proverbially at comments of this style –, 'excuse me, lads, it's 1987, we don't need unions', 'I don't need any old bastards telling me what to do, it's the 1970s not the Victorian era' – anyone putting 'the year' or 'the decade' into an argument fundamentally misses the point about progress or lack of it and it's supposed exact lineage with the passage of time. People will tell you that this country 'has lurched to the right' in recent years and there are others in this country that will say that it's been brought to its knees by Lefties in the past few decades. I don't know what decades or years have to actually do with it, especially when Christianity is 2,000 years old, but one would have thought the time to say that we didn't need Christianity anymore was during the time of those crusades where people were murdered en masse and not when you've just watched another sanctimonious episode of Songs of Praise with that vicar woman that used to be on Gogglebox. On a side note, a mate of mine did say that he cannot stand this 'decade-isation' of events and I replied 'yes it's such a bloody 1970s attitude'. He eventually saw the funny side, but looking back the quip wasn't worth it.

Anyway, back to the populist anti-Christian debate. I don't have statistics to back this up, mainly because I don't think statistics can ever convey the feeling that you feel living in a certain time from a certain perspective, but I do remember the rampant and militant atheism certainly in Britain from about 10 years ago. I can confidently say that it isn't anything near those dizzying heights anymore and it barely even gets a mention even from the fanatics from a few years back. I liken it to how punk never seemed to get talked about from about 1981 from the pseuds in the music and entertainment press like it was something we should shut up about like Cromwell or the Spanish Inquisition, then a discernible time after that (mid to late 80s) those same pseuds, when they realised how culturally important it was looking back would bore you at length of how they were massive Sex Pistols fans when they were teenagers and how they spat and puked everywhere in 1977 because they were so angry and everybody from the establishment was frightened to bloody death of them — 'but hey we were punks and the old guard just didn't understand us' aye right, Jeremy.

The God Delusion was certainly a book of its time. It was a slow burner not a fast burn like a sinner in the pits of hell (sorry I must stop joking!) but it crept up. In 2006 when it was published it wasn't immediately making its mark; however, by 2010 it had sold more than two million copies and from what I remember had a massive effect on the general populace rather than the very small amount of well-read folk that live amongst us. Women were buying it for their husbands at Christmas as a surprise like they were getting them a pack of their favourite craft beer or some quality underpants. I remember some real meat and potato two-bit idiots quoting stuff from it to me 'proving' that there was no God. It's weird because I'm sort of an atheist myself, much like Richard Dawkins, but I must have had a Christian face or something due to the queue of non-believers ready to give me their bit of evidence to prove conclusively that there's definitely no God. It's okay, I believe you!! Now I'm not going to ever get the time back after listening to your dogma about there being no God, and ironically enough it's all very precious this passage of time malarkey because as you say when this life finishes there is definitely NOTHING. Perhaps as compensation can you, I don't know, pay me some money now, you cunt?!!

Very quickly people got on board, particularly in America where a lot of them haven't really sussed the organised religion con in the same way Europe has. The two people I can think of were Brian Eno and Ricky Gervais, two people that were perfect champions of it looking back, not too high brow but very much go-to figures in the pseudo intellectual world and ironically enough both British. As it happens, I like both of them two as great entertainers, creators and original thinkers of their respective times, but come on, the book wouldn't have had quite the appeal if Suzy Quatro and Roy Chubby Brown had talked it up.

One of the passages quoted to me by more than one person was the amount of miracles that had 'really taken place' at Lourdes down the years. As you can imagine this gleeful recitation that I got was from two elapsed Catholics determined to cite this particular chapter and to tell me about the lies of the RC faith and the Pope and Daniel O'Donnell and all the other dreadful people involved in a church that I don't really care about either way. As you can imagine 'the real figure' was very small, almost miniscule, proving once and for all etc etc.

The other 'bombshell' was that the Romans apparently wrote everything down but there was no such name of Jesus Christ in those times so there you have it, no Jesus Christ, no religion, you are wrong, Christians, stick that up your arse, and when you've finished sticking it up your arse and start crying while admitting I was right!

There's so many things I'm sure we can all say to this; I don't know, Galilee at that particular time wasn't the best of areas to ascertain whether indigenous birth registrations were very accurate due to a certain King Herod putting every boy to the sword under the age of two, perhaps the whole Jesus comes under a different name in that period of time hence Yeshua bin-Nun and other such similar suggestions his name might have been. Maybe the Romans at first wanted a dangerous bloke like that written out of history altogether; they certainly haven't been the last people to do this — there's three off the top of my head. The idea that there was no record of a Jesus Christ from the Roman census system seems to be a bit of a downright naff section of a book if you ask me!

What Dawkins has done to his credit is he's acknowledged in later editions that some of the big theories he came up with have been debunked. His crude observation that 95% of DNA is 'junk that does nothing' was disproved and it's accepted by science that every bit of DNA does something. As a zoologist one would have thought that that was his specialist subject, so if he's wrong on that why listen to him on anything else? Is that harsh? Maybe it is, and as I say I'm not a scientist but a mere swearer for a living; however, I'm not the one that flung my opinions round like a muckspreader in the first place telling people that I was dropping a bombshell.

Apparently the 'selfish gene' that is covered in the book has been largely debunked as well, which he has also acknowledged and has since said that the role of science was to have been questioned and ultimately proven to be incorrect.

A couple of years later, would you believe Dawkins was spearheading a campaign to have the King James Bible taught in every state school and was quoted as saying "A native speaker of English who has never read a word of the King James Bible is verging on the barbarian". He went on to say that he didn't want it there for moral reasons but for the great work of literature that it was and that it didn't seem right that there are copies of Harry Potter books at state schools but no copies of the King James Bible.

I don't know what that says to you, but to me it turns out that Dawkins is a big auld snob, rather than this non-secular freedom fighter, and finds his very readers to be heathens yet he's happy to have their money — who gives a fuck if the book is a bit scattergun and not that accurate, it's fooled a few of the Hoi Polloi, so much so he can get himself some nice holidays and a big house. Of course I don't believe that last sentence, I just went a bit tabloid for a laugh, but when he's debunking the Bible as a bit of fiction then the question must be well your daftie book is as well, isn't it?

What these modern-day pilgrims progress in reverse folk don't seem to get is that religion is very often a private and personal thing for some people and their own religion is a great time of comfort to those people during times of stress or bereavement, loneliness etc. in the same way lighting up a Regal King Size is to others. Do they still make those particular tabs? I've no idea but you get the principle. Not every Christian is a tub-thumper; in fact, unlike most other faiths, it has a discreetness and a private-ness to it where, in most cases, you might not even notice the person who is participating.

I'm not wanting this book to descend into 'hey brother live and let live' cos that's ultimately not what it's about. I'm an opinionated bloke myself who likes the pantomime of debate, but you know sometimes folk just won't let it go when someone has a personal belief or superstition and they feel that they must autistic-ally point it out like they just bloody well have to in case the klaxons go off in their head that they didn't mention to a Christian that Christianity is without doubt the worst thing in the history of humanity. I don't know, these people are suddenly emboldened because a zoologist wrote a book that was admittedly well written and not turgid like something by Karl Marx, but a just a stocking filler book all the same, with not that many pages debunking an Abrahamic religion, and they begin behaving like a weird Christian with you but in a sort of parallel universe. As I hinted earlier, a lot of the readers and voluntary missionaries on behalf of the book were no doubt from very dogmatic Christian households, a good number of them would've been elapsed Catholics and it was their big chance to finally stick it to nuns and priests from their own early life that would be long dead now and ironically enough not able to cry in shame or get their comeuppance or even to acknowledge that they were all wrong because as the militant atheists are always at pains to point out, there's no afterlife, no heaven and no judgement day for those people. Their baddie status just exists in the head of the angry Christian-hater.

It's common knowledge that priests and, I should imagine, all members of the clergy whatever flavour aren't frightened of these rabble rousers. I've heard it said from them many times 'I'm not worried about people who hate the church, they're not the problem, they hate the church because they're actually frightened of the church, I'm more worried about the people who are bored with the church'. I've quoted this to many a militant elapsed catholic atheist and the thick fuckers still don't get it — 'Yeah too right we're all bored with these paedos with their frocks on telling us what to do and look at them with their dress on, what are they going to do at their sermon? Do the can can in front of their altar boys that they're no doubt getting sucked off by etc etc'.

Meanwhile the real enlightened just have a nice lie in after a hard week then wash their car or get the Sunday papers then go out for lunch or watch a bit of Motherwell versus Hibs on BT Sport while getting ready to go down to the pub to catch Arsenal against Everton.

The biggest irony of all of this (and I've hinted at it earlier) is that when I've been cornered with these anti-God sermons from the newly enlightened, they mention The God Delusion and that it's a great book and it blows religion 'wide open' and you should read it. I then would ask them when they read it, they'd say that they'd just read it recently after they'd got it for Christmas. Sometimes there are no words required.

POLITICS

I bet you've heard this phrase before, 'To be honest I don't like any politicians, they're all the same as far as I'm concerned, they're all just out for themselves but I tell you who does talk sense'...the name that immediately gets brought up is someone very right wing, in these dark divisive days it's invariably someone like Farage or even more depressingly Tommy Robinson or Jacob Rees-Mogg.

It's very much, to use a phrase you hear these days, 'truth bombs' that according to the supporters of these rabble rousers, sensitive people don't like to hear. Apparently saying the unsayable is what elevates blokes into great statesmen, it doesn't seem to matter if it's wildly inaccurate what they're saying, or embellished somewhat, or only half of the story and half of the facts (the facts that suit their own narrative) are revealed, as long as it's passionate and it's a 'truth bomb' the supporters of these 'sense talkers' don't mind. You never hear or read that the voice of sense is coming from someone with... well...sense, someone who can see the presented problems from both sides and therefore is looking at finding a solution. No, it's always someone who tells you how their lot are feeling, 'people are sick and tired of this' that's a common one and 'The British people have had enough'. As soon as whole populations en masse are being spoken for as in 'people', 'the British people', 'the taxpayers', 'working class people in this country', you should in my opinion avoid the person using those phrases at all costs.

The thing that grinds my gears is people seeing politics and seeing getting things done as piss simple, that the only thing in the way of a new road or planning permission for the retail units etc. is a jobsworth whose sole purpose in life is to just put the mockers on things. That red tape only exists because people are twats and love red tape, that bureaucracy is there because people at the council get a pay rise if something is delayed, that everyone is on the make and that if only we could start a new council with the 'sense talkers' then all these delays would lift immediately and everything would fall into place and there'd be no corruption and the humming of the bees and the cigarette trees etc.

In my hometown of Blaydon on Tyne, the whole place at the end of the 1960s through to the mid 1970s got bulldozed and destroyed because a whole load of blokes from the council with far too much power decided to bulldoze it just because they could. If only there had been red tape and banning orders and listed building status in those days, my wonderful hometown wouldn't have been reduced to a big roundabout with a flyover and some faceless retail units replacing a bustling community. People were moved, pubs were pulled down, shops were levelled, and supermarkets and a pedestrian walkway were installed with a big fuck off car park that turned into a ghost town at night because no flats had been installed on top of the supermarkets or housing of any kind in the vicinity. It was that classic horrific 1960s utopian vision, the ones with the prospective photos of smiling people parking their car and shopping with the new buildings in the background that went wrong very quickly, even quicker I'd say than even the harshest critic would have envisaged, and along with the Beeching cuts on the railways turned Britain into these aforementioned ghost towns so beautifully articulated in the number I hit by The Specials in 1981.

I'm certain that this was all to do with people riding roughshod over people's views or their fears of their hometown being demolished. I'm sure there was many a palm greased from the council to developers and vice versa. Obviously, I can't name names or even present you with facts or the minutes of the meetings, but it was at the very same time as the Poulsen affair with T Dan Smith at Newcastle City Council, the sorry episode where money was handed over by contractors to win council contracts to install shitty flats with damp and dry rot and all the other bad things that go with cheap 1960s high rise flat housing. Both the people involved (council leaders and the contractors) were jailed and Newcastle was left with some dreadful social housing and a West End that had been totally wiped out in the name of progress. T Dan Smith wanted Newcastle to be 'The Brasilia of the north' and ended up in the nick.

Again though, according to the modern day arse talkers, that's apparently exactly what we need now, a whole load of local Kim Jong Un types who'll decide on a whim to knock stuff down, build shit in its place, have a radical building policy, re-route roads and decide that there's a new town replacing the old one, and then realise they've made a terrible mistake half way through and change their mind when it's too late. No doubt those very people that were championing these do-ers before would be the very ones after their blood when it all ends in tears.

Look at the trams in Edinburgh — apparently according to the modern-day arse talkers they were shit and a waste of money, then they were great and should have been brought in years ago and why were the original tram lines taken up in the first place, then it was a waste of money again that could've gone on better things. I don't know what they feel now, I think that they're just trying to gauge public opinion and then act on it like they were a visionary.

The little I know about leadership and what I've been told by people is that you must keep your nerve. You can't just change like the wind with what your long-term goals are or totally abandon a strategy because it wasn't instantly working, you can't just regret a recent employment recruitment and want that person out that you were championing just before they were hired. The country seems to be full of these on-a-whim morons these days with short termism running through their DNA. It comes at a time where people are living longer and you can see change even in half a lifetime if you're patient.

'The fact that we have food banks in 2020 is so tragic, in fact it's a disgrace'. Who is disgraceful? Who should feel disgraced? Don't just leave it there and say that it's a disgrace, tell us why. I think just outlining the symptoms and not the cause and sticking a year on it or saying 'in this day and age' to make even the year superfluous is enough for people. Or rather it's enough for people of polarised politics to agree on something. I'll put them together. 'To think that here we are in 2020 and the UK, the fifth largest economy in the world, and it's come to this, I mean surely in this day and age people shouldn't be relying on food banks?!' There you are I've managed it. Yes it goes round the houses a bit and it sounds bloody excruciating, but it's a big bold comment that, when you analyse it, doesn't mean anything beyond the outrage. It doesn't tell you what side you're on, how you think it came about and what your solutions are to mend it.

THE PATRONISING 'LEFT'

You could almost write a 600 page book just off the back of a fag packet where the 'left' have told you how to live, how you're wrong, how you're offensive, how you're patronising people without even realising it (a delicious irony that is lost on them as they tell you this), how your views are apparently dangerous, naïve, rabble rousing and countless other adjectives that denote that you're a baddie and on the side of the bad lot, boo hiss.

Of course, what is 'the left'? I would probably describe myself as left wing in that quite simply I feel that people that have lots of money should pay their fair share in terms of yearly taxes and those with bigger salaries should pay a fraction of their salary like everyone else into the tax system and that's it. Yes, it's as 'unradical' as that. I personally don't think that that's in any way left wing but I'm sure the popular press would regard me as some kind of Trotskyite or least of all a head in the clouds naïve idiot for thinking that some sort of system could work properly. Those newspapers, of course, for anyone who didn't know tend to be owned by people with offshore companies that pay precisely fuck all into the system and haven't throughout modern history. The left just because of their part exposé of this fact then gets squarely bashed daily by your Suns, Mails, Expresses and Telegraphs, and that's the left from from someone like me right through to a real radical that insists we nationalise every industry in the UK, get the whole world to not trade with Israel, give the Falkland Islands back to Argentina and wants to force everyone to work less than 32 hours a week because they apparently deserve it.

THE SELF RIGHTEOUS

The politics of the self-righteous can come from all political sides and all political agendas. It covers a rainbow of views but the one thing they all have in common is that they always accuse their political opponents of being exactly what they are. The self-righteous always have the whiff of people not researching though or being ignorant of the full facts. It's not ever wilful ignorance, it's more that they're deaf to criticism of their side, or that there's clearly a reason for the criticism and go to the ends of the earth to prove that, and that normally involves discrediting the opposition or the whistle blowers, basically whoever is doing the criticising of, in their eyes, their untouchable cause. They believe that the other side are the 'baddies' and can never give credit where credit's due or have any kind of balanced or nuanced opinion on a subject from free school dinners to the Israel/Palestine conflict. Being a conviction politician is something that you have to be very good at or at least have knowledge in abundance in order to follow through with it, mainly because I'd say there are two sides to every story and I can only think of a handful of conviction politicians off the top of my head who actually are of that level of intellect. The two I can think of have, believe it or not, both been leaders of their own political parties in recent years, namely Iain Duncan Smith and Jeremy Corbyn. I'd say though that both men would sink their head in their hands when listening to some of the self-righteous that champion their respective general sentiments.

THE HEALTH FASCISTS

Ah yes, the health fascists with their self-righteous indignation at anyone that doesn't follow their Ladybird book of a healthy life. How many times have you heard a version of 'I think smokers should be denied NHS treatment'??? Oh dear this one again! 'Yes, they are a drain on NHS resources, treat the non-smokers first', I'm sure you've heard many versions of this one. It's tempting to say where do you start, but it's quite easy where to start and finish, and in my view it boils down to three salient and succinct points without getting into the fine detail or the statistics; these are:

1. Smokers contribute to the economy greatly by the huge amounts of duty on a packet of cigarettes or any kind of loose tobacco along with filters and papers. They're taxed enormously as everyone knows and we'd all miss it if this yearly tax disappeared.

2. Smokers, especially heavy smokers, tend to not get to retirement age, they die in their early 60s as a rule so they don't need the state pension which accounts for about 40%

of the total annual welfare bill. Basically, smokers don't get the pension.

3. From what I've read down the years, a smoker will unfortunately go very quickly, they will get very ill with the cancer and will not need much in the way of treatment because their illness will unfortunately last weeks rather than months.

When you put this argument to one of the health fascists and ask them if they eat chips, cream cakes, red meat etc. and ask if they like to drink alcohol regularly, they'll insist that that's different and it doesn't directly cause death when of course it very much does.

Another time the health fascists had a field day was when slightly lardy TV chef and someone who always seems to look like a 1990s Britpop anachronism Jamie Oliver decided to tear into the school dinners and tell us all via television that they were a national disgrace and that he was going on some sort of campaign to make them affordable and that turkey twizzlers were definitely off the menu for good!

Has there been an improvement to people's health? Is there a generation of people in their early to mid-twenties right now who are discernibly fitter than the people some five years older than them? I'd venture that they're not because the real problem to me is social media and PlayStation, not the percentage of turkey that might be in a twizzler. Now that's me maybe getting political and a bit partisan, but in keeping with this book it's that bandwagon jumping and lack of nuance from people that just decided one day that the one problem with children's health in the 21st century was one specific food item and not a fundamental problem with children's relationships toward exercise, amounts of food, the culture of takeaways, eating after 6 o'clock at night, determining certain food outlets being cool, food and soft drinks companies sponsoring sporting events, films, the gaming industry etc. I could go on and I'm sure you could as well, but oh no, they watched Oliver one night on a much heralded TV programme back in 2005 and they were converts to twizzler blitzkrieg.

THANK GOD FOR OUR WONDEFUL NHS

Americans call it a cult, some people pop their head above the parapet and say that we should perhaps move to an American model of health insurance, then of course our old friends the self-righteous blow a gasket and tell people to wash their mouth out with carbolic soap for even thinking such sacrilegious thoughts, never mind sharing them. The NHS costs too much money, it's not a bottomless pit, can we not prioritise spending and encourage people to do certain things so we spend less? These questions are seen as some sort of Dickensian mill owner talking and that they are so beyond the pale they don't even merit an answer.

Although I'm not a fanatic, you can probably tell where my politics are based if you've read the bulk of this book; however, I do have an admiration for one of the most Conservative sayings of recent history and that is that you can't just throw money at a problem. It gets done in the public and private sector, very small to very large businesses invariably fuck up by doing it, as do many organisations from snooty artistic institutions to charities, community collectives and sports clubs. A big drive to make people sit up and take notice, an almost suicidal spend of Wonga to drive home what a brilliant concept or product they have that will, they think, catapult them amongst the big boys and leave their rivals trailing in their wake normally ends up an unmitigated disaster and a signal that big spends will never ever happen again for any years that they have left as a company which are now numbered due to the financial folly that's just gone.

The same can be applied to the NHS. The people that insist that 'all the lottery money should go on the health service' I guarantee would be the sort that would spunk millions away daily by running the NHS wrongly, the ones that think that all our beloved health service needs is spending to be quadrupled and people will suddenly live longer, that waiting lists would be slashed, that we'll smile more and everyone will have a wonderful quality of life. You think this paragraph is simplistic? Well, I'm only reporting what a lot of people seem to think. It's not a simple left/right thing either. The amount of so-called Conservatives who start lip quivering when going on about the NHS is alarming. It's like the Dylan song 'With God on Our Side', people seem to think that the caring and the selflessness along with the duty of care as well as fair play belongs to their lot and with it the wonderful NHS whereas the reckless selfishness belongs to those other bastards who use the NHS but don't care for it really. However, the one thing they both think is that nurses are all wonderful, the NHS is wonderful, doctors that work in the NHS are wonderful and the other people who don't deal with the life and death part have varying levels of wonderfulness but don't top trump the wonderful nurses who are of course all wonderful.

'I tell you what, they should swap the hard working and wonderful A&E nurses over with some of these so-called Premier League footballers then we'll see what happens', yes there'll be deaths, mate, needless fucking deaths. Deaths that could've been easily avoided if someone with a bit of poise and composure as well as cool judgement was in charge of hiring at the NHS like there is at the moment, instead of a knee jerk populist idiot like yourself.

Imagine some poor soul coming into A&E and it being reported to the ward manager that they'd died because the nurses didn't know what to do when they went into cardiac arrest. 'How many times have I told you, start working on him with your hands, get the defibrillator, use that and then get aspirin into them, who the hell snogged him and gave him Calpol?'

'Erm well, you're not going to believe this, but it was Mo Salah and Harry Kane.'

'What the hell are they doing here?'

'Well, you know when the self-righteous took over the country and they said that they should swap the hard-working nurses in A&E with the so-called premier league footballers?'

'Yes, well I didn't think they'd carry it through, I mean where the hell is Joyce?'

'Joyce?'

'You know Joyce, your boss, our matron who would oversee such things, you know Joyce, overweight, obsessed with cock humour, smokes like a chimney but she's very good at her job, where the hell is she?'

'Ah, she's playing for Tottenham.'

'What the hell is she doing over there?'

'Well, you know when the self-righteous took over the country and they said that they should swap the hard working nurses in A&E with the so-called premier league footballers?'

Meanwhile, as you can imagine 63-year-old Joyce is having a nightmare at White Hart Lane.

'Mark up, Joyce.'

'Eeeh, mark up yourself, big cock.'

'You've let your runner go again.'

'I'm 63 you know and I'm 17 stone, anyway fuck yous, I'm away for a tab.'

STATISTICS (PARTICULARLY OTHER PEOPLE'S)

A wonderful tweet from Nigel Farage on 4th July 2021 read:

In 2014 when I said 250,000 people would come from Romania, I was met with outright hostility — especially by the BBC's Nick Robinson and James O'Brien of LBC.

Well so far 920,000 Romanians have applied to settle in the UK.

You won't hear this much on mainstream media.

Well, the first thing that you can do is research that statement. It'll take you all of 30 seconds and you will find that it's not accurate. There are a few conflicting figures, but there are about 400,000 Romanian nationals in this country give or take, and it's people who are here legally, like you know they were invited to help with a labour shortage you know like those 10 pounds Poms in the 1960s in Australia. Some other reports put the figure at around 800,000 but these people are actually 'British nationals'.

Also, some of us remember Farage simply adding the actual total population of Bulgaria and Romania together and telling us that it was something like 26 million people ready to come over to Benefit Britain all those years ago. I don't remember him quoting a manageable 250,000 figure where people might respond with 'well that would be quite good especially if they're all young and ready to work, they could really pick up the slack on our industries where we need good people'. No, apparently it was all of Bulgaria and Romania and they were ready to clean out our wonderful NHS and that's why it should be privatised.

No doubt people would howl with solidarity at his gloomy picture due to these correct figures; however, look at the wording '250,000 people would come over' and '920,000 Romanians have applied to settle'. Yes, a very different thing isn't it, applying and actually coming over. No doubt I could apply to be on a mailing list for a Rolls-Royce Silver Shadow or for the first commercial flight into space. Perhaps I could apply to be in the Grand Order of Water Rats or apply for the job of head of comedy at the BBC. I'm fairly sure I won't get these positions though. It seems though in Nigel Farage's followers' worlds, applying and actually achieving seem to be the same thing.

I don't think you'd hear this much on mainstream media

because it doesn't hold any water, just as you don't hear very much on mainstream media about the Alton Towers Smiler crash being an inside job, or that Enid Blyton faked her own death. Basically, mainstream media doesn't bother with stuff where the facts are skewered and juicy figures are put up but aren't really conducive with the real statistics because the person putting the figures up was banking on people not bothering to differentiate from 'applying' to 'coming'.

To be fair to Farage, he's probably got a load of nougats believing this statement hook line and sinker because they've not read the tweet properly, but the statement I suspect wouldn't even get past an assistant researcher at the BBC as they'd do that annoying thing of asking him to show what he means by applying and how it differs from coming and if he could then produce some figures on the actual amount that have actually come over in the past 11 years or so. Certainly, the net figure per year would be a massive help. What's that? It's not all that remarkable? Oh, I see.

THE AMATEUR ACCOUNTANTS

Well I suppose we've touched on this earlier, but I am fascinated by those that use the word 'bankrupt' when talking about a country, especially a free country with a currency that's used around the world and people come here from around said world to shop, get their children educated, buy our handmade cars etc.

'I'll be honest I think the country is going to go bust,' they say like it was a small engineering firm on an industrial estate. You can see the other countries coming in and buying our machines as two blokes with overalls on are sweeping up and having a bit craic with the asset strippers. 'Where's the British population?' a German remarks. 'Ah they're all getting rehoused round the world while the country's in receivership, mate,' one of the blokes with overalls on replies.

I remember when it was reported that Mexico were the world's biggest debtors. However, people still dealt with Mexico, people left the place and arrived there. Their airports and docks were still open. Countries bought their exports and they still had the World Cup in 86 despite being the world's biggest debtors and having recently suffered from a massive earthquake. It wasn't boarded up and on the boards were posters for The Lady Boys of Bangkok or a 'club night'. No country goes 'bust' as people think. Yes, to use domestic financial affairs as a metaphor is useful, but it would be much more accurate to say that some countries get endless IVAs that they have a long time to pay off. I'd also say even as a layman to this sort of thing, and without any research, that the Democratic Republic of the Congo, for example, probably doesn't need to pay off Zaire's debt because technically it's a different company managing the same strip of land.

Just have a look at the markets: people can get access to the FTSE 100 or the German DAX or any of the exchange market rates in an instant, whether it be on your phone, tablet or on your telly on one of the many dedicated TV channels. You can find out how lawnmower companies are doing in Bolivia in an instant, or whether gold is on its usual upward spiral, or whether it's in the doldrums as it occasionally is between spurts. There's no message going on people's personal stock market portfolio app saying 'Some countries have recently gone bust, if you've money in any of their companies then you have our sympathies but we do not provide a money back guarantee'. Despite many a commentator claiming that it is, the stock market isn't an arcade in Vegas.

WE CAN'T AFFORD IT

We can't afford what? It? What is it? Whether it's healthcare for Afghans, or sex changes for those woke trans people, the argument tends to go down the road of us not being able to afford it. It means that the racial or potentially homophobic debate is avoided if one can start a sentence off with 'lovely idea but we can't afford it' and all other potential obstacles don't even need to be attempted due to the 'we've no money, therefore the idea is now dead in the water' technique. It is said that we were 'skint' in the 70s, that the IMF bailout was not only embarrassing but it meant Britain became 'the sick man of Europe' and other such cliches, but even the most partisan Tory orientated book, column or journal of any kind talking about that decade always has to grudgingly admit that people's living standards grew considerably. People's aspirations changed and people began to really live a little in the 1970s. There's an oft repeated phrase that goes 'for working class people the 1960s started in 1971' and I'd say that was accurate. No matter what the official line is from the pseuds that tell us what a ghastly time it was back then and the ones that said that Corbyn and his mob (they tend to refer to his followers as something resembling kangaroos) would have us catapulted back into the 70s, the fact is that it was the start of the sort of prosperity for working people that they've come to accept since. There's no way we can ever go back to one-week paid holiday a year, a few days in Blackpool/Southend/Largs for a summer break and you can only have a car if it's a company car. Apparently though, all this frivolity we can't afford because some bloke down the pub said.

Can we afford some new motorways? Can we afford new rail lines? How about a subsidised integrated transport system where the bus/train prices are slashed by about two thirds and petrol prices stay the same so it's a better option to take the greener options and not trudge down in your gas guzzling motor on your own; however, the park and ride schemes are there so you can park your car for free out of town and take the light railway into the city centres? I suppose we can't afford that even though the benefits, be it financial and environmental, not to mention the individual stress levels being avoided because no one is in a traffic jam, would be seismic. No, the idea of us paying out a load of money for something great like this over a long period would be folly and would be far better spent on HS2 or Trident. Have you noticed how things get more editorial as the book wears on?!

BRITAIN IS FULL

Another one where people tell you the arbitrary amount and that amount is the amount that they've just set. I remember a London cab driver telling me this — 'they can't come in, Britain is full' he said at his wits' end when the latest immigrant speculation was being played out on every tabloid that day.

What is full? Is 67 million 'full', was 55 million 'full' (that was the population when I was a kid). Back in the Victorian era (say the 1840s) there was much less in the way of people, I believe it was something like 20-30 million. Was it empty back then? Did it need a surge of people to bolster things up and kick start the industrialised economy? The reason I ask was because the Irish population at the time dropped in the 1840s to about half its size, I wonder why that was? Was Britain 'full' then?

It's a fairly obvious one, but immediately after World War Two Britain may have had overcrowding in cities but there was a massive labour shortage due mainly to young men coming home in boxes during the conflict of 1939-45, some not even coming home and others coming home minus limbs or with permanent debilitating problems. People from the working classes in the decade before that (the 30s) were seriously underweight and weren't in the position to do hard labour which a day's work was back in those days. Britain may have been 'full' then, but it was full of sick people, through I may say no fault of their own. The only option was to advertise for the jobs people wouldn't or indeed couldn't do. Jobs were advertised in Jamaica, Trinidad and indeed all of the West Indies, also the new independent Pakistan and India recently partitioned and in 1947 free of British rule. As a result, people from these colonies over the next 20 years arrived and started making a living in very distinctive industries. In the north of England, they tended to work in the mills of Lancashire and West Yorkshire, in the capital, they migrated toward London transport, and of course lots of educated immigrants became doctors and nurses. Perhaps the place was just three quarters full then or was it full? Define full. Is it so no one can actually move or is it just full in the sense that you don't WANT anyone else coming in??!

THE
FAIRER
AND
SUPERIOR SEX
BUT
HOW DARE YOU
PIGEON HOLE
US

FEMINISM

'HOW MANY FEMINISTS DOES IT TAKE TO CHANGE A LIGHTBULB? ...ONE'

Oh, how I laughed when I heard this one. Ironically enough it was on Annie Nightingale's Radio 1 Sunday night show in the late 80s and in a series of changing a lightbulb jokes that were sent in to her by POST back in those days. Yes, feminists rightly or wrongly were a bit of a joke in the Thatcher days, even on a programme hosted by the first ever female Radio 1 DJ and self confessed 'wicked witch of the wireless.'

I love totally outdated concepts that make up jokes like this, they're like wonderful antiques. The idea that a feminist could only be so as a result of strong feminist type symptoms is what makes it funny for the wrong reasons to start with!! The idea that only butch women were standing up for women's rights tells you how far we've come as a society. It's great to think that feminist traits to watch out for were apparently practical maintenance skills and a good example of this being comfortable around a man's preserve of changing light bulbs. That must have been a tell-tale sign that you weren't dealing with the average bird here.

The thought of getting a bulb out of the bayonet cap because it was not transmitting light anymore and replacing it with another one made you some sort of North Sea oil rigger with muscles like garth. It also meant that you were a bit weird as a woman to understand this complicated concept and that you wouldn't get it all messed up in your pretty little head.

Feminism and Lesbianism were sort of the same things in the 80s in the eyes of most men and women. I remember one woman in the late 80s/early 90s telling me that she thought that men got a raw deal. This is a woman who was about 40 at the time and would be over 70 now. She was a 'strong' woman that had solid but radical left wing politics as her philosophies and morals, and stood up to blokes at every opportunity. If she's still alive now I'd love to meet her and ask if she still thought that men got a raw deal. All I'm saying was that it wasn't better or worse back then, only different.

I remember in the wonderful days of corporal punishment in school, me and a few other lads in my class got bent over and walloped by the teacher for terrible misdemeanours like 'talking during a lesson' and other such acts of school heresy. A few of us were in the smacked club. One time the teacher in question (Mr Armstrong class 2A, Blaydon West Junior

School 1978-79) asked me to come to the front. I brought my book, he told me with great pleasure that he didn't want my book and pushed my head forward and whacked me as hard as he could a couple of times on the arse in front of about 30 other children all in silence at this point. As I walked back to my chair trying to pretend that it didn't affect me, that was when he chucked in his editorial: "You're putting the whole table off". I didn't know whether the putting the whole table off was with my talking or just my very being. I personally think he just fancied smacking a boy that day because he hadn't for a while. This wasn't the first time in that school year I was whacked by him, and it was always at the front of the class like I was to be made an example of for talking in a lesson or something. It was like a kitchen sink version of 'She' with Ursula Andress where she gets people to toss the tribesmen into the boiling water for 'stealing'. As he was into belittling children with homophobic remarks, I'd love to have had my moment and minced around him in his nursing home and called him Ursula Andress, but alas my day never came.

The year before that I'd done quite well and never had a second thought of what sort of kid I was — looking back, I was a bit of a swot and quite boring. After this particular school year (2nd year of the juniors which would nowadays I think be Year 4) I was now convinced I was a bad lad, quite naughty and a bit of a waster along with other lads in my class, all down to a boy-hating teacher that was probably a bit of a closet.

The striking thing was (but none of us questioned it) no girls ever got whacked when they misbehaved — maybe they were too precious and delicate to be hit, which of course is sort of sexist in a weird, seedy, slightly child abuse type of a way. We (the boys) were fair game, and it seemed to ramp up tale telling and dobbing the boys in the shit from the girls who I think did derive enjoyment out of their male peers getting physically abused in the public arena of the front of the class. They all laughed at the teacher's crap jokes and revelled in him saying how pretty they all were and that the boys were no more than low life future factory floor fodder despite them being eight years old. I look back and teachers of that ilk should definitely have been investigated. Obviously there was no hard drives in those days, but it did make you think what else went on when they were at home and during their LONG holiday when they clearly took such delight in pummelling small boys about a third of their weight, most of the time getting them into compromising positions and made to stay still when they did it.

#metoo was a wonderful exposé of men and how badly we've behaved over the years, but to see the teacher of eight-year-olds give the boys dreadful shit daily (when he wasn't hitting them he was telling them how stupid and gormless they all were) and suck up to the girls, for me seemed to bring a poisonous hatred and a divisiveness between the sexes that wasn't there before junior school right to the fore. It created a ghetto on either side and years later when everyone from those formative classrooms are now fucking each other, the battle lines between the two genders had been well and truly drawn.

Aye, the teenage girls were there to be humped and dumped, they were there to be given a good seeing to, but they weren't our friends for fuck's sake!! It had been seen to when we were kids that we were both so incompatible that we must never close rank and be one. I can't speak for people that went to all-boys schools, I personally find that weird, but they were determined to divide and conquer in our school and I bet in all inner city schools back in the day.

To bring it all to the spirit of this book, it's the fact that people rail about things without even knowing the history of it.

I'm sure if people could have beaten the feminism out of lasses they would have, but it would have been against the code of honour of 'never hit a woman' which is a laugh anyway because the real unwritten rule was 'never hit a woman in public' and that is becoming clear from what is coming out now. Perhaps the code of honour if I'm being honest was 'never hit a woman, unless it's your wife and it's in the house.'

MEN BASHING

I like men bashing, it's a good form of humour, as is women bashing. Is bashing too strong a word, what with domestic violence still being rife in 2020-21? Surely in this day and age ribbing would be a better word (yes I deliberately put the year in to accentuate it even more even though it doesn't mean a fucking thing).

Jokes about men being lazy, about men being incompetent, being too set in their ways, procrastinators, sex mad, and stuff about them not listening and resistant to change is all fair in love and war and within that awful phrase 'the battle of the sexes.' 'Men are from Mars And Women Are From Venus' was a best seller and I bought it for a joke I did at the Edinburgh fringe many years ago. Despite just using it (by holding a copy of the book up) for one fairly weak joke during August of 2009 or something, I'd bought a paperback copy but I'm proud to say I didn't read any of it. You might be thinking I fit into the stereotype of the many things I'm railing about in this book as in I'm a bloke who is harping on about something I've never read, but honestly, from the people who've read it and enjoyed it to the quotes that I've been unfortunate enough to hear from the book, I don't feel like I'm prepared to devote the time to reading the bastard; I'd rather take my dogs for more walks or get the car washed or something.

People did, however, see it as their bible; I'm tempted to say (without any research to be fair) that as Venn diagrams go I bet some of the people who salivated over The God Delusion by Richard Dawkins were keen crusaders on the musings of Men Are From Mars And Women Are From Venus. Some of the stuff I've seen quoted are so obvious and so of a standpoint of the very clichés and hack stereotypes of men and women, even the most mainstream of stand-up comedian would say 'come on, mate, that's a bit obvious.'

Stuff like this spills over into discussion programmes — have you seen for example an average edition of the daily lunchtime magazine/discussion? show 'Loose Women' on ITV?!! They talk without irony about 'love rats' and dreadful 'two timing' men in the public eye (normally some herbert that was once in a boy band or some tit that was in a soap opera for a while because THEY ARE ALL MEN); however, when it's a woman having an affair behind her husband's back there's some sort of explanation to follow... this is one I heard from one of the ex-Nolan Sisters member endorsed by the others 'she was probably sick of her man not paying her compliments or telling her that he loved her because she was getting on a bit and maybe she wanted to find someone else to pay her the compliments and that's why she'll have found love elsewhere, and it's not nice when you get older and your man doesn't pay you compliments etc etc.' Ha! I love it, best of all they don't know they're doing it and to be honest when they're giving pelters to middle aged men at least they're not doing what they love the most and that's being horrifically right wing, which seems to me by watching is to be some sort of prerequisite to be a regular.

Of course one can scoff at populist shows like that, but to try and find some sort of solace on the radio doesn't seem to bring you any joy either, as I experienced myself once. I was listening to BBC Radio Newcastle one night while cleaning the kitchen and doing the dishes (I deliberately haven't used a traditionally female role as a backdrop to hammer home my annoyance at reactionary women by the way!) and there was a woman discussion programme going on. You could tell by the posh voices (sort of Geordie posh if you know what I mean) that it was meant to be light-hearted but trying I think to lean more toward the Radio 4 type of audience rather than the ITV daytime market share. Anyway, they were talking about 'men' surprise, surprise! and how they (and I bet you've heard this one before) always complained that they were dying when there was very little wrong with them and that women had to put up with much worse pain but just got on with it and if those men had just a bit of that sort of pain you can imagine how much they'd complain then ooooh it would be unbeeeeeerable, yes the usual clichés. There was much laughter and a general murmur of agreement and a few bits of anecdotal evidence about each of their own husbands just to make the whole observation completely true and put to bed. The host at this point jumped in (as all good hosts of debates should) and said that men were more likely to put off going to the GP's or the hospital because of serious symptoms of pain leading to life threatening situations and this was borne out with NHS statistics. This sparked one panellist to explain in a long and winding road type of a way why this was the case, it went something like 'I think when it's a trivial thing men will whinge and complain and tell you that they're dying, but I think when it's a serious thing when you should try and do something about it, and something that women will be straight to the doctors about, men will ignore it and think if they forget about the pain it'll go away.' Fucking hell, lads, we can't win, can we!

I was once at the chemist's trying to get something for my aching limbs, sore head and with it sore ears and sore throat. I tend to get throat/ears problems whenever I get laid low with a cold virus as I think I'm susceptible in that department, I think due to hereditary problems just like everyone is, with some as you know it goes straight to their chest, sinuses etc. The reason I was at the chemist was because I was working and doing a five-day straight road trip down south and staying in hotels in between, I basically needed something to keep me going so I could keep working to, you know, pay all the bills, but also I like doing my job as a stand-up and I didn't fancy feeling sorry for myself at home for five days whilst earning nowt. Anyway, the woman in the chemist said 'what's the problem, is it the man flu?' Anyway, I stared her out for about five seconds and then explained the situation again in almost a whisper so as to accentuate the point. She got on with it and found me a suitable over the counter medication to help me cope with the impending misery over the next few days that I'd be trying to work through. She could tell that her man flu joke hadn't landed very smoothly that day.

The 'man flu' was a thing that used to get said that encapsulated this observation about men complaining about being very ill when there was nothing wrong with them at all. I don't know where it actually comes from? I'd say it comes from a few wankers that do complain about that and a feminist writer decided that those few wankers were 'men' and lo, one joke that would be done to death was born. It used to get tossed around by women quite a lot and it was mildly amusing at first, but then after a while I began to feel embarrassed for intelligent women that I knew. It seemed that their alleged wit was being exposed as being no better than a couple of Theresas and Jeans in the queue at Greggs.

There is an Australian feminist writer (well at least I think she is) called Kathy Lette that seems to turn up not even on Loose Women but on cheaper versions of it on Channel 5 complaining about men most of the time, or when she's not doing that, complaining about The English being so uptight and stiff upper lipped not like the salt of the Earth Aussies (another cliché klaxon) and she seems to have re-hashed the same joke many, many times when she's appeared on these programmes. The joke being about equal pay for women, it is thus: 'women in Britain don't have equal pay and that we are still getting concussion hitting our heads on the glass ceiling. We're also expected to Windex it while we're up there'. She has used that 'joke' on pretty much every chat show she's been on, not only that it's used on interviews she does with every broadsheet or tabloid. Google her and you don't need to look far for her Windex classic. It's like she's proud of it or something?!! She's never really been on one of the high profile chat shows as she's very much selling her wares at the pound shop by being on cable type channels, but nevertheless you'd think she'd have written a new feminist joke by now. I'll be honest, I don't even know what Windex is, maybe that exposes me as a penis wielding woman hater but there it is; I tend to use soap and water, and newspaper is a good agent to clean mirrors and the inside of windows as well, not aware of this Windex character in all honesty. Personally, I wouldn't like to clean an overhead window — I might catch something like man flu! However, if there's only women been up there previously then I'd probably be okay seeing as they're immune or something.

AS A VICTIM OF SEXUAL ASSAULT

'As a mother', ah right so the childless women have to sit this one out, do they? Like they haven't got a partner for the Dashing White Sergeant so all their pontificating means nothing on this one and it's only the ones who have given birth who are qualified to make comments on this matter. I've never heard women say things like 'as a rape perjury instigator' or 'as a serial liar that embellished stories to such an extent that my ex couldn't see his kids anymore which led to his suicide', that one doesn't look good in a self-righteous discussion.

WHY ARE THERE NO WOMEN ON THIS LIST?

This one is my favourite in the times we're living in. Yes, that'll solve the world's problems, acceptable quotas! There's no women on this list because no women applied. 'Well find some that don't even want the post and then give them it' they'd probably say because woe betide a list that only contains one gender, what the fuck would we do.

What about why isn't there a woman James Bond? I always like that old chestnut, it stimulates yet another in my view pointless debate. Well, when Ian Fleming wrote the childish escapist nonsense that bears no resemblance to the real world, he meant for the character to be a posh English lad that went to Fettes school in Edinburgh hence the slight Scottish brogue, cue the film role was played by Edinburgh man Sean Connery. From what I've read that was the reason. But why isn't there a woman James Bond now? I don't know, it's fictional anyway. Quotas, balancing up, even for stuff that isn't real — has the world gone mad? I mean, for example why isn't there a bloke Mary Poppins is something you never hear. Why? Because it would be fucking ridiculous, that's why. Why isn't there a black James Bond? I've heard that one as well. Honestly, I give up. What about why isn't there a black Doctor Who? You must have heard that one. I always say to those people, 'look when William Shakespeare wrote Doctor Who he intended it to be a scatter brained eccentric posh English man and most British people with Afro-Caribbean heritage weren't even around in this country at that time, not even Othello as he was from somewhere in Italy or something.' I do like to answer moronic questions with equally moronic answers because they can't then say 'you're just being silly now' because I could reply to them 'well you started it'. Why aren't there more women CEOs? I don't know, why do you want women to have such ruthless horrible jobs anyway, you might as well say why aren't there more women asset strippers, more women high interest money lenders and loan sharks, it seems the loan shark business is dominated by the guys, why aren't there more female pimps or women people traffickers. Sometimes it looks better if the horrible blokes have certain jobs, doesn't it?

I remember the supermodel Naomi Campbell complaining that there weren't more black people involved in the modelling industry. Is that a noble statement or is it just naïve because the modelling industry as everyone knows — and I don't think I'm speaking out of turn here — is completely designed to exploit people, it's abusing young ladies in the main, just to earn quick bucks, it's rife with exploitative greed, it's corrupt, the industry is synonymous with abuse, rape, harassment, endemic sexism and of course chucking people on the scrap heap because they're <insert young age> and they're finished. Is it a case of 'hey I wish my brethren could get on to that cushy number', the whites have been making money out of young women with eating disorders for too long, let us have a turn at exploiting them.

PATRIOTISM, NATIONHOOD AND NATIONAL PRIDE

THE SIEGE MENTALITY

Aye it's an old trick; however, the siege mentality is, shall we say, more manufactured nowadays to create loyal regimentalism from foaming at the mouth supporters. Nowadays if your position is under threat and people are trying to make you keep your mouth shut, it means that apparently you're getting to the authorities, that people that are standing by your cause are somehow ahead of the curve and not only that, on the right side of history and sticking it to the man. It's a much better look being a freedom fighter than someone sent out to do the establishment's dirty work. When it comes to national pride or rather the supposed suppressing of national pride, the English and British nationalists use the siege mentality so much, it's difficult sometimes to find what they're actually proud about in the first place.

Everyone hates us, no one likes us, but we don't care, there's people out there determined for us to fail, you'll have heard all of those ones before. The paradox is, those types of statements tend to come from the very people that hold all the cards because they're part of the establishment, you know, the ones making the actual decisions, but they use this con trick to make it look like they're some sort of plucky independent underdog. On a side note my favourite one is for the modern day 'shock jock', you know someone in the spirit of perversely one of the biggest cultural figures of modern times in my own humble opinion, James Whale (the veteran late night radio talk show host), to declare that 'there's people out there trying to get this show banned' when in actual fact those spurious claims normally amounted to a couple of old Methodist ladies writing letters via second class post to the provincial radio station complaining of the lack of moral standards from the host and that someone said bum live on air the other night or something like that.

The favourite one from the St George's flag wavers is to claim that they're being squeezed out by an imaginary politburo suffocating their English identity through stealth like the slowest moving python in history.

THE BLOODY LEFTIES THAT RUN THIS COUNTRY

What I always find laughable is that whenever a general election comes around (to a lesser extent a national referendum or local elections) and the right of centre free market policy party almost always comes out on top, there is much merriment and vigorous celebrations from the righteous right wing supporters, much ha bloody ha and many a 'stick that up your left wing arse' type comments. These same people though that were partying hard celebrating their liberty and freedom then spend the next 4-5 years complaining about how the lefties run the bloody country and how the wokes/snowflakes/rah rah right ons/do gooders/politically correct idiots won't let you do anything. It's about how you're 'not allowed to say anything these days', how they 'tell us what we can and can't say and what we can and can't do', apparently they ban Christmas, they ban St George's Day and ban any kind of patriotism and kill all joy and freedom enjoyed previously by the decent hard working people in this country. I thought your lot won? I thought your lot ran the country? You know, the (mainly) men with the clipped posh voices that went to Eton or Harrow or some other school with its own crest and hymn theme tune surely can overturn this woke madness? Perhaps you voted for the wrong lot? Maybe if you'd voted for the party that was interested in protecting your working rights, the ones that didn't want you to work in a zero hours contract or that want the derisory minimum wage to go up to a much more manageable level, you may not be complaining so hard? Maybe it doesn't matter what party you vote for, the Diwali festival taking place in your local park is here to stay? Maybe you're wrong, have you thought about that?

Lefties running the country, have you ever? If real lefties ran the country — and I mean real lefties — you'd have more freedom than ever because believe you me they wouldn't know what was going on under their nose, they'd be frigging useless at running the place and you could have a Trafalgar Day, a World Cup 66 day and even a Jim Davidson day, and they wouldn't have a clue how to stop it. Perversely you should vote for the lefty parties every time, eventually it'll give you your freedom. I know it's impossible though because you're always drawn for some reason to posh men in suits and monocles telling you what to do.

ST GEORGE'S DAY

What a terrible political football a supposed day of celebration has become due to the tiresome street politics sloganeerers, the poorly educated, the arse talkers, the cultural Marxists and the people with no original comedy material types. Firstly, we have to hear every year that St George wasn't actually English at all. You get the smarmy social media posts from the pseudo intellectuals every year, 'happy St George's day let us celebrate the Syrian stroke Isreali with Greek and Turkish heritage shall we'. It seems that they want to put one in the eye of the bigots by pointing this out annually, but to me they're just cementing my summation that these people are always left puffing and panting when there's the need for an original witty remark to be made, a stark reminder of how these people would be bereft of anything to say if they couldn't parrot other people's caustic wit. The first time this fun fact was pointed out to the nation it was probably interesting and food for thought; now the idea that a semi mythical person may not have been from the country he was supposed to be mythically from is hardly a scoop. In fact, it's rather boring.

Quite why that pisses off patriots I don't really know, but it seems to irk with not just your BNP, NF and English Democrat types, but the so-called 'acceptable faces of the right' as well like BBC comedian Geoff Norcott the self-styled Conservative supporting funnyman who insists that you know that he's right of centre politically despite coming from a council estate. I don't understand, even though he's at pains to tell us this, why the council estate thing is a big deal at all when you look at the Brexit vote — the fact that the aforementioned nationalist movements tend to poll very well there and as someone who didn't come from a council estate but went to a school where most people came from one and whose grandparents lived on said estates and most people I worked in factories and building sites with came from there — it wouldn't surprise me that someone from that part of an inner city suburb would foster right of centre views. He once did a big filmed piece online at the end of his tether about people that went on about this Israeli/Syrian thing re St George. Why get so upset? No one mentions the fact that he allegedly killed a dragon which as far as I'm aware is the most unlikely part of the story, not where the bloke was actually from.

I mean bloody hell, getting het up by a semi mythical person and where other people claim that he hails from is mentally ill, isn't it? imagine if there was a story breaking in Greenland that Santa Claus wasn't actually Greenlandic, in fact it turns out he wasn't even Innuit, it was probably based on St Nicholas from the 4th century (Greek, they get everywhere) or is based on Germanic folklore, indeed his name is Dutch as in 'Sinterklauss' so in fact he's probably from the low countries, he's not even Scandinavian. Maybe a Greenlandic 'lefty' would tweet it, you know maybe a modern undergraduate bohemian type from Nuuk University (if there is one) and the whale blubber, fish gutting hard line Innuit working men got aggressive about it, took to the streets and claimed that there was more money spent on bunting for the celebration of Sir Donald Soper's birthday for the very small Methodist community based in Sisimiut than anything for the Norse Gods and with it Santa's rightful home on the North Pole Greenland. Do you know what, I bet the aforementioned doesn't happen at all in Greenland because its 58,000 or so people, unlike a lot of British people, have more important things to worry about.

Anyway I digress, the biggest thing I feel that gets pushed on St George's Day, April 23rd every year, is that, and I bet you've heard this one many times, 'people have barely mentioned it'. Here's a few more 'on St Patrick's day you couldn't move for coverage, today it's like we're embarrassed by the whole thing' or 'the jocks have got their day, the paddies and the taffies have got theirs, it's a shame we can't have our day without being labelled racist'. It's like these people look forward to people not mentioning it so they can mention it and tell all that no one has mentioned it.

Then there's these claims that the local council spent X amount of pounds on the Diwali festival last year but none at all on the St George's Day celebrations, despite constant lobbying by the local Union Jack bring back hanging group and that there was an Irish flag flown at X council's offices on St Patrick's Day but not on St George's Day and that there was loads of mentions on BBC Radio somewhere about Ramadan but not one mention of St George's Day by the clearly left wing host and the left wing producer who clearly had a left wing agenda; and so it goes on.

Would these angry people be happy if it was a public holiday? Would you be happy if it was a public holiday? I wouldn't object at all to be quite honest, anything for another day off and as it's normally quite nice weather on April 23rd it might do the English tourist industry the power of good with a massive spike in hotel bookings and bar takings for 'English weekend'. English ales would do a roaring trade from the many off licences I have no doubt, as would pork pies, tea and I don't know, toad in the hole or whatever English fayre is served up by restaurants for the day. Maybe coach companies would clean up and also outdoor marquee installers as well as bands and entertainers to provide some sort of order of service to the national feast of civic merriment. I think a holiday to celebrate some chap who slayed a dragon and with it celebrate everything that's English is surely a good thing and a real tonic to the hardworking folk that live on this island.

Imagine though if it happened? As in made more of a big deal, leading by example from the top starting of course with said public holiday? Of course, every few years when it fell on a Saturday or a Sunday we'd have to have the Friday and the Monday off respectively which I'm sure no one would mind. What do we do though? One thing that the British don't like — and I think we're more bolshy than most first world countries about this — and that's being forced into doing things or forced into behaving in a certain way, be that grief, fun, devotion, celebration etc. Yes, we sometimes do jump at the chance to go all subservient on the Queen's birthday or a bit jingoistic for VE day anniversary commemorations, but in general we don't do coerced enjoyment as easy as others do around the world.

As I've intimated before, the angry mob would paradoxically hate it if the whole day or whole weekend went England crazy, for the simple reason they'd have nothing to feel the victim about, they wouldn't be able to use that claim about how the lefties won't let them celebrate. No one is objecting to them putting a flag up in their garden or from an enormous flagpole on their front wall, I've seen far too many of those when I've driven around to know that no one has complained. However, they always seem to feel that they've hit the jackpot when (normally assisted by The Sun) they've found a news story from some part of England where a decent bloke who wanted to put a flag up for the World Cup or to celebrate a royal baby was forced to take it down by the town council. The fact that we live in a part of an island with something like 57 million people in that said area, I'd wager that there's bound to be a bit of friction over somebody's massive St George's flag somewhere. Also, you have to question the people that are the most vocal about how St George's Day isn't acknowledged and what they're like when they're not complaining about specifically that.

I know that if I was in charge, for example, of BBC programming for April 23rd and there was a modest but not huge budget thrown at it, I'd have fun and I'd make sure we were all in for a televisual St George's feast. Surely the daytime programmes could be St George's themed, have a live programme where celebrities pop by and have a chat, you know a St George's based cooking recipe done live by one of those almost cliché ridden Englishmen Jamie Oliver or Hugh Fearnley-Whittingstall, then some English type films in the afternoon, you know The Wind In The Willows or Passport To Pimlico. In the evening you could have a lot of great stuff on. Maybe at 7pm the Prime Minister could address the nation wishing everyone a happy St George's Day and then there could be a live concert for a couple of hours on BBC1 with choirs singing Gilbert and Sullivan songs as well as orchestras belting out Elgar and Benjamin Britten as well as poetry from Kipling and other such populist literary types done by contemporary English artists. To make sure we've got highbrow culture covered on BBC2 we could have a more beard scratchy St George's Day, maybe a documentary on what it's like to be English in the 21st century and interviews with all types of members of the English community and its multicultural diversity. Perhaps a programme after that about the history of St George's Day and how the sense of Englishness was different in the past, then maybe a programme about William Blake or CP Snow. Perhaps on the red button or on BBC Sounds there could be a heated debate about what it means to be English with different firebrands all chaired by Fiona Bruce or David Dimbleby. It might be a good thing to go out on a high on BBC1 with one of our great records enthusiasts like Gideon Coe, Mark Riley or Danny Baker to extol the virtues of English popular music and its influence round the world. I'm sure I've only scratched the surface, but that would be fine for the first year. Surely one or two of these shows could be repeated the year after, and new ones could be made like a documentary about English sports and pastimes and a live show from a seaside resort or a cricket pitch or somewhere else quintessentially English, a BBC2 documentary about English humour and music hall comedians and how distinctive the English sense of humour is followed by an English comedy routine of the year show hosted live by one of our great modern comics with several other English comics on the bill, then show that classic Likely Lads episode where they don't want to know the score from the Bulgaria v England match played that afternoon, England F.

I very much enjoyed writing that previous paragraph and I'm enthused by it all. I'm convinced a day of televisual broadcasting would cheer people up, even if most were out in the pub enjoying themselves and not bothering with the telly, but I'm sure to those that watched it would send them back to work in a better place the next day without it ever getting mawkish or sugary like American patriotism. However, the angry mob wouldn't be pleased with this sort of thing at all, they'd be appalled at such kowtowing to the cognoscenti, having to listen to the experts coming out with big fancy words and trying to tell them what it's like to be English. The programmes would be slammed by the popular press the next day telling their readers that they were being patronised and it was more woke communist nonsense from the so-called BBC.

To them they'd just want wall to wall war memoirs all night and documentaries on The Battle of Britain, The Battle of Trafalgar and maybe a documentary about how history has been revised to make the English look bad. If they had their way you'd have The Queen doing a special St George's Day Trooping the Colour, Land of Hope And Glory on a loop in the afternoon for an hour, two world wars and one world cup, a documentary about Enoch Powell, Rule Britannia on a loop at 10 o'clock instead of the news, and to end the night loads of old racist comics doing jokes you're not allowed to say anymore live from a working men's club. Maybe we should just do that, give them what they want, make them happy — at least they might stay in and leave the outdoor enjoyment for all the nice people.

YOU CANNOT SAY OWT THESE DAYS

Or the double negative, you cannot say nowt these days, or depending upon what part of the UK you're in, you can't say nuffink these days or ye cannae say fuck all these days. You get the idea. Yes, apparently in 2021 you're not actually allowed to say things in modern Western countries. I don't know exactly what that means because once again in keeping with the mood of this book, the people that chuck these types of bold statements out like Olympic Discus throwers are invariably ones who aren't backwards at coming forwards in saying a lot of inharmonious and quarrelsome things in the first place, invariably badly researched and inaccurately sourced. Also, you very rarely get people challenged on these big statements. What do you mean you can't say anything these days? Well of course what they mean is you can't say stuff about people's race or their racial stereotype, derogatory things about people's sexuality or gender, you can't bully people or belittle or patronise women, or talk about people in the wrong context when it comes to their physical state or their mental state. It's that, isn't it? I might've missed a few out, but generally you can't be racist, sexist or homophobic without someone taking offence.

I've been guilty of all three in my moderately long life, some more than others and some of my faux pas (there's no plural for the phrase) I've done fairly recently. Sometimes I feel that I never learn. I've got things wrong, I've been a bit cheeky and familiar with people when there's no need for it, I've been a bit rude and a bit cutting and dismissive over groups of people I don't know enough about, and I've been in the company of many others who have horribly insulted people and communities on an industrial scale and I've never done enough to stop it. It's always going to happen, and I don't expect people to instantly apologise for it. The cultural totalitarianism from the culture police gathers evidence together, builds up a portfolio of rotten things this person has also said in the past and damns said person so they can never work again because they don't measure up to the so-called exemplary standards of not being offensive — I'm aware of that; but not being allowed to say anything anymore?! No, I doubt it, mate. The prime minister has been caught making horrific and offensive or unfortunate and ill-judged comments (depending upon how slightly right or moderately right of centre you are) and he still gets away with it and at the time of writing this bit (April 2021) is about nine points ahead in the polls. So much for not being allowed to say anything!

The other phrase that makes me laugh is 'you've got to be

careful what you say these days'. The reason that it raises a wry smile rather than a guffaw is that the person making the statement implies that what they're wanting to say is obviously not very nice so they have to qualify it with a statement almost asking people listening to the story if they're on board with offensive words. One of my favourite jokes — and it's a visual one so it might not work in book format — is 'How does every darkie joke start'? The punchline isn't any words, it's just the joke teller checking to his left and right to confirm that there's none in the room before looking like he's going to launch into said offensive joke about that particular ethnic minority. It's very much a Stanislavsky breaking down the fourth wall joke but it's a good one though. When people say 'you've got to be careful what you say these days' or 'you can't say anything these days' really means something like this: You've got to be careful saying things these days that are sort of disguised as jokes but are really forms of abuse to people who aren't as powerful to fight back in the room, because there's a real chance sadly that there might be a white working class bloke who's a good fighter and built like a brick shit house who won't stand for this kind of racist filth anymore and will knock you out'.

IN THE OLD DAYS YOU COULD SAY WHAT YOU LIKED

No, you couldn't. Certainly not in the public broadcasting forum you couldn't. I'll not bore you with copies of legislation or directives from television commissioners, but basically you were governed by laws made by watchdogs, be it BBC watchdogs or the ITC (the independent television commission) to keep in line what you do on television and there would have been something similar censorship-wise for the radio. At that time, you actually had to have (get this) permission from a living person if you wanted to do an impression of them! People like Queen Victoria were okay, but not the current queen or prime minister. This changed in the 60s with That Was The Week That Was and people like Willie Rushton and Peter Cook doing impressions of Harold Macmillan and the like. I'd say every prime minister or indeed high ranking government minister has been impersonated since these times and probably the most famous of these impersonators doing the voices of the government and the opposition as well as all the celebrities of the day being Mike Yarwood from the late 60s to the early 80s.

The other thing you couldn't do was swear. It was very strict. Not only were swear words a no-no, but so was 'blue material', anything that was vaguely alluding sexual practice was out. Indeed Max Miller was banned from the BBC in the 1940s for this joke:

Max Miller – I was walking along this narrow mountain pass – so narrow that nobody else could pass you, when I saw a beautiful blonde walking towards me. A beautiful blonde with not a stitch on, yes, not a stitch on, lady. Cor blimey, I didn't know whether to toss myself off or block her passage.

He was banned from the screens for five years, five bloody years for that joke!

Indeed not long before this and indeed not long after the Second World War, a double act called Clapham and Dwyer were banned for six months from BBC Radio after this joke on the Light Programme:

"What's the difference between a champagne cork and a baby?" asked Clapham. When his sidekick said he didn't know, back came the response: "A champagne cork has the name of the maker on it."

Apparently, a page of their material was missing so they were just ad-libbing and this joke which obviously wasn't vetted by the gatekeepers just slipped out. Only it didn't, it was caught attempting to slip out and it cost the pair of them dearly.

THE REAL SNOWFLAKES

Of course, this you can't say anything anymore tribe tend to follow it up with 'in case you upset a snowflake' or 'some woke is going to get upset' – woke seems to be a noun sometimes as in you are 'a woke' as opposed to someone being woke in the verb sense where it's sometimes used. I'll try and get a few of them in together, here goes: 'I'd like to say what I think but as you know there's always some woke snowflake that's going to be triggered and they'll get me banned by getting in touch with the PC police and get me cancelled with their cancel culture'.

I find it ironic that people call the so-called triggered people snowflakes because they've supposedly stopped them from saying what they like when being angry and frustrated that someone has taken offence with what you've said is kind of snowflake behaviour in itself, isn't it? Telling all and sundry that you're not allowed to say anything these days is equivalent to whingeing on to the ref because you're apparently not allowed to foul people on the football pitch these days. Without any sense of irony whatsoever, people say things like 'why do people get so offended by so-called racist jokes? I've never been offended by racist jokes'. Well, the answer tends to be in the make-up of the person launching this kind of diatribe. They tend to be white and the racist jokes in question tend to be toward West Indians, Pakistanis, Indians and West Africans, who make up the majority of the ethnic minorities in this country. Of course you're not going to get upset or offended by a joke that's not actually knocking the community that you belong to! Same goes for Irish people being thick and Scots being tight. In the archetypal Englishman, Irishman and Scotsman joke, which is a classic rule of three in the mechanics of comedy, normally the first person to do something as a reaction to the bizarre situation the lads have found themselves in is the Englishman who tends to behave as you'd expect a normal person to despite them being in a tight spot. The Scotsman tends to follow that logic afterwards and then the Irishman comes in and misses the point and says or does something hatstand but normally where he's taken something literally or misjudged a metaphor for reality or tries to cleverly get out of something but inadvertently frames up the sentence to make things even worse. Inevitably, our friends Paddy and Mick in that classic two hander joke where sometimes they're builders but other times they're undertaking leisure activities, are both a bit idiotic — normally one will say something stupid and then the other one would say something stupider, but they're making sense to each other; both of these thick paddies tend to be on the same wavelength.

The Paddy and Mick analogy is an interesting one. Sometimes I feel when the joke teller is telling a story about what utter fuckwits they are in the form of the script of the joke, they inadvertently make them out to be brilliant thinkers that are taking down society with their surrealist answers to red tape or parroted dictum from a person in low grade authority. Instead of their idol Thatcher smashing the trade unions, if only Paddy and Mick could've done it by taking their union leaders totally to their word and making it impossible for them to impose any kind of industrial action. Here's a great one: Paddy and Mick go into a pub at dinnertime, eating sandwiches, the landlord says 'I'm sorry, lads, you can't bring your own food in here' so they swapped sandwiches. Genius! Joke teller tells this and might as well follow it up with 'Goes to show how thick they are; however, the more I hear it, it's two perceptive Irishmen instantly rendering someone's power redundant by not breaking the rules but volleying their rules back at them by giving them an instant lecture in semantics by the sandwich swap. I don't suppose adding this bit on at the end would give you a bigger laugh than the punchline in a busy concert room to be fair, even in an Irish Club!

ENGLAND, BRITAIN AND THE UK – SAME THING, ISN'T IT?

As an Anglo Scot I could always see this but when I explained it to other English people they didn't understand why one would get upset by very small discrepancies between someone saying England and meaning Britain. A Scottish person can see the difference, but it's even more obvious to a first generation English person or someone who has moved to England.

To many an English person they always see Scottish people as having a massive chip on their shoulder, many a phone-in on many a radio station is dedicated to 'chippy Scots' who won't let it go, but then in the next sentence those people that berate the Scots talk freely and ignorantly about England and what England have achieved as a nation over the years.

How do you feel as a Scot when your family has served in the British Army and your ancestors have fought in Gallipoli, at the Somme, El Alamein, the D-Day landings, got captured in the jungle by the Japanese and had many other moments at almost fabled places during the 20th century to then see a whole load of young men running amok on the continent chanting 'Two world wars and one world cup'? What about the amount of times that people talk about how England used to make loads of cars and that England has achieved so much despite being such a little country, that England has the best trained army in the world and how England once had a massive empire?

A mate of mine once said (half joking but a massive English patriot) that he thinks that Scotland should have their independence and then England should invade, just making the whole country a 'massive England'. The flaw with this proposal is that most English people just think of Scotland as 'Greater England' anyway. Loads of bloodshed would be avoided by behaving the way they do already and telling others that it's part of England. Indeed, during the referendum debate in 2014 the talk was always how they subsidised Scotland. I always thought it hilarious when you got some embittered angry soul from the North East of England, South Yorkshire, Cumbria, Lancashire and many other ravaged areas stepped up to the plate to declare that they were 'fed up of subsidising the Scots'. Oh, the irony. These parts of England are basically 'sick notes' and have been for the last 40-odd years, propped up mainly from the city of London and our stock exchange and everything that goes with it. The government finds it hard to tax everyone, but lots of these insurance companies that make fortunes every day are taxed and the money pays for universal tax credits to swathes of people on Northern council estates, small government departments, parts of the DSS and lots of other central government sponsored offices where people turn up every day in their lanyards to look important and do a job that could probably be done in the capital, but the fear of mutiny and the whole of the North of England being some sort of swamps and Badlands area is very real, and the best thing to do is to throw these bastards a bone now and again.

I wouldn't bore you with figures because this isn't the SNP manifesto, but the city of Edinburgh is a very rich city and has a yearly budget that dwarfs probably every city in the UK bar London; there's also fishing, whisky, farming, tourism and of course North Sea oil and gas that keeps the Aberdeenshire area very well and although lots of the country has its social problems, Scotland's natural resources and other assets it has going for it strikes me as evidence that should it go independent, it would have no problems looking after itself.The idea that it's propped up by England is only sort of a quarter true, and even then it's ambiguous at best. I'd say some of the Scottish cities are supported by universal credits, by giving people money when they're not working and paying stamp and tax basically. Perhaps without looking at the figures this is evident in the city of Glasgow and perhaps true in the less than salubrious parts of Fife and Ayrshire along with the West Lothian area (all former mining regions), but other areas can look after themselves as they're more affluent. This of course is the same in England

and indeed in Wales. If Scotland were independent, to use right wing terms, junkies, layabouts, single mothers, jailbirds and other wasters would get their money from Holyrood as opposed to Westminster, and the gaslighted British people can blame some other group or some other region for there being no money for other services. It'll be the 'somebody else's' to blame and that they're sick and tired of subsidising the 'somebody elses'.

I'M SICK AND TIRED OF HAVING TO APOLOGISE FOR BEING ENGLISH

I love this one! It's a phrase that normally rears its head on phone-ins and it's invariably sparked off by a football World Cup. It's of my opinion (and it's only an opinion but I feel I could bare it out with anecdotal evidence) that the football World Cup has sort of had its day. It's either in a period of terminal decline or it's just having its barren years before hopefully coming back in the future as the iconic tournament it was between I'd say 1970-1998. There's lots of arguments as to why it's not got the spark it once had, and as I say I might be looking at it from the nostalgia lounge, but I think most football fans would agree that the mystique and the anticipation of seeing brand new players from around the world that you'd never previously heard of alongside the idea of watching live football matches on the telly for a solid month when all you had was edited highlight packages for the previous four years made for heart racing excitement. That and the fact that it featured one or two countries from the British Isles meant that it felt like a real treat for the flat cap football fan to watch some crazy Soccer festival of the best in the world shaping up against our plucky but not as cultured lot in the baking heat in what for them days looked like another planet, but where people in the noughties thought nothing of visiting in their gap yah!

The other reason why it's not what it was for me is because back in the day it was a tournament for football fans primarily and then some extra folk with a passing interest in the beautiful game that would devote their lives to these matches played on the other side of the world for a June and July once every four years; people would stay up late or wangle an afternoon off just to catch Brazil v Sweden in a group 3 game that afternoon. The excitement was palpable and non-football people complained that they couldn't watch their soaps or the news because football was on 'morning, noon and night' even though it wasn't and they couldn't move for football analysis even though there wasn't that much of it. It went wrong though in my opinion because what previously had been a football feast for the purists gradually became a signal for an out of control nationalistic monster to surface that couldn't be chained up.

One night before the 2006 World Cup started in Germany, there was a special programme on Talk Sport about Scotland's dislike of England and the debate was a question of whether it was justified hatred, reciprocal bigotry or just plain old fashioned jealousy. Cue a whole load of people with no grasp of history, be it military, social, government legislation or even football history, chucking their money in as to why there's conflict between the people of the two footballing nations. It was quite embarrassing, but more importantly it all lacked humour and a sense of the fact that it's just a bloody ball game at the end of the day. Later on in the tournament as the pressure was mounting on an England team that once again had been hyped up to triumphantly come home with the World Cup but in reality looked like an also ran, there was a late night phone-in on BBC Radio 5 Live about the strange practice of the celtic countries wanting England to lose as though this was some kind of new phenomenon. The mood of the nation wasn't great as England had stuttered through the group games and people were pinning their hopes on them boring their way to glory from the last 16 right through to the final. Some of England's patriots were at breaking point, other parts of England where local clubs are of more importance were indifferent, and in Scotland and Wales there were premature smirks of laughter being picked up. Anyway, this sparked another whole load of buffoons to ring this particular show, but in this case with more plummy accents that (call me cynical) didn't sound like your average football fan. The immortal line was broadcast from the first caller "do you know what" he said in a Hugh Grant voice "I am sick and tired of having to apologise for being English". When you hear someone with a colonial, upper middle class voice say something like that, my first reaction is come on mate you've never apologised about anything, let alone being English!

The calls continued with more and more posh people – "Fair enough support your own country but I've heard that Scots were not only not supporting England but they were actually cheering for the other team to beat us!" Ha ha is that so, mate?! Never heard about that before! Obviously the 'Scotland World Champions' sports headline in 1967 and thousands of them invading the pitch and digging the Wembley turf up in 1977 has passed you by then? And what about the immortal line in 'Ally's Tartan Army' by Andy Cameron 'We're representing Britain and we've got to do or die, for England winnae be there cos they didnae qualify'. It seems that the angry posh nosh English nationalists had no understanding of football history and the rivalry that goes with it. It is what has kept the working classes divided for years in my opinion and stopped them storming Buckingham Palace. While they're tearing into each other about their respective football clubs, they neglect to realise that they're given such a raw deal by the people who really run this country, but the hoorays haven't grasped this and sometimes fail to realise what their greatest strength is, and that is their apathy and ignorance of such things!

It was comedy gold though hearing this parade of naïve Tim Nice But Dim breakdowns on national radio as I sped through Nottinghamshire at midnight on the M1. It was as if they thought that these Scots needed teaching a lesson and some sort of gun boat be deployed to come up the Clyde to Glasgow and fire some shells into the treacherous bastards.

For fuck's sake, no one is asking anyone to apologise for being English, no one is seriously in this day and age (there's another one) taking to their beds about how people were hard done by in the wake of the battle of Culloden or Flodden Field, I mean these things took place 300-400 years ago, or in Bannockburn's case 700 years ago! Scots with flags of Remember Bannockburn printed on them should be taken with as much of a pinch of salt as a bed sheet with 'Spread Em Ray' written on it in 1977 at Wembley referring to Ray Clemence letting the ball go between his legs from Dalglish's shot at Hampden the year before that gave Scotland a 2-1 win. It's football rivalry, I refuse to call it banter (I hate that word, it's so bloody twee) because as a football fan it's far more than that, it's huge, it's satire itself, much bigger than any parlour game shite about the balance of payments or some new legislation from Whitehall where the people making the jokes might as well be the same people making the laws as they all went to the same schools. I'm sure that all those people will be very proud to be English and I doubt I'll hear an apology even though they're allegedly sick and tired of it.

THEY'RE SELLING PARAGUAY SHIRTS IN GLASGOW

Never happened. No evidence of it ever happening. England go to World Cup tournaments that Scotland don't qualify for and there's a story that 'insert popular sports shop chain of the day' have run out of shirts of England's first group opponents in Glasgow, I presume to hammer home the bitterness and partisan nature of the chippy Scots who want anyone but England to win the trophy. However, there's absolutely no evidence to ever back up the claims, no quotes from the store manager, no copy of the sales chitty, not even cobbled together photographic evidence of a rail with Paraguay XL stickers on the top and a big gap where there was said shirts, which of course they keep stock of regularly in their Sauchiehall Street branch I shouldn't wonder. Imagine how easy it is to fake that up, it wouldn't take a lot of effort!

To put to bed this whole myth, I'll just put forward a stereotype that the very people making these claims would enjoy: there's no way a Scotsman would spend his money on a shirt that he's only going to wear once, there's no way he's going to part with £55 to prove he hates the English. He'd far rather buy a £3 flag saying 'Remember Bannockburn' or 'Doon Wirra English' or some other such cliché than buy a Paraguay strip. Total and utter shite, but a small paragraph in The Sun or the Mirror saying that you can't get a Paraguay shirt for love nor money in the Scottish central belt because they've all been bought up by small minded jealous tartan bigots is enough for great swathes of people south of the border to say 'there you go, I've always said this, just a country with a massive chip on their shoulder and I say let them have their independence because in a few years' time they'll come crying back to us etc etc.'

HAVE I MISSED ANYTHING?

You can tell when you've spoken to someone who knows little, it's not at the point where they're very poorly furnished as regards facts on the subject, it's the cocksure way they conduct themselves beforehand. Very often when they say things like 'I tell you the problem with this country', you know what I think the trouble is.' I've just had that with someone on the weekend of writing this bit (September 2021) — his opening gambit was 'the trouble with comedy these days' and then a contradictory, messy argument with what looked like himself about what you can and can't say. No nuance, no classic examples of what he means, no symptoms to back up the cause, nothing. Just a few soundbites in a confident voice.

He also did that classic thing of saying 'extreme right wing people and extreme left wing people annoy me, you know I can't stand extremists of any kind, I like people like myself who are in the middle' — yes, it's apparently these non-moderates who try to get things changed that are the problem. When they are invariably changed for the better, him and his ilk claim that his lot, the people in the middle that did precisely fuck all about it, forced about the change and the extremists as he calls them just fannied about and made a fool of themselves.

Anyway, I feel I've come to the end of my stream of consciousness about different institutions and conventions and how the uninitiated but confidently uninitiated talk with great knowledge on these things. Have a look and see if you can see examples of 'Buddhism and such rubbish' and send me an email about it on gavinwebster@btinternet.com

You're welcome.

POSTSCRIPT
– COVID THE SECOND
LOCKDOWN AND THINGS
OPENING UP

I write this in the Autumn of 2021, a weary world, a world that now doesn't seem to like frivolous behaviour, a light-hearted view of current events or any kind dark humour unless you're on a designated dark humour page where it's encouraged to not do humour but merely hurl insults at the people you disagree with. As you can imagine, it's all a bit touchy feely and people seem to like a lot of feelgood stories and selfless behaviour. However, it's all mixed with a cynicism and a mistrust of anything supposedly feelgood. It's very much a daily paradox in Britain 2021. Feelgood stories but only from the official sources. No indie feelgood stories, we'll tell you what you need to be proud of or what you need to have a quivering lip over.

Of course in 2020 it was a lot different: 100 year old men got knighthoods for walking around their BIG house 100 times, and nurses and doctors and well everyone that was connected to the health service got a round of applause every week. People were ticked off when they attacked the government because the prime minister was apparently 'doing his best' and we were coerced into all being tolerant and nice, but like it was the Khmer Rouge in charge of the tolerance and niceness.

We now find ourselves once again in a country of division. The whole Brexit thing hasn't gone away and as a result of empty supermarket shelves which is clearly augmented due to a pandemic, the Remainers that still haven't let things go are having a field day posting up pictures of nothingness in Tescos where there was once food. They'd love to tell us that people are starving to death in this country, but that genuinely would be bollocks, so they have to go for the much softer consumer angle about how there isn't 'the choice' that there used to be. Not being enough types of tahini in the supermarket isn't exactly the unemployed of Jarrow marching to London in 1936, however much they spin it out. Anecdotal evidence isn't something I really want to push, but I've not seen any empty shelves in the supermarkets I've been in, and the small food shops seem to have everything they need in order to sell.

You get the impression the whole Leave/Remain thing will wane over the next few years; however, the vax/anti vax row seems like it will run and run. I don't reckon that's a straight 50-50 argument like the Euro or the Scottish debate, it's more (and this is a massive guess but it's in the spirit of the book) like 90-10, but of course the vocal minority like to make themselves heard at every twist and turn and the majority either ignore or roll their eyes or begin debating but back down when confronted with a frothing at the mouth conspiracist.

What of the anti-vaxxers? Well to be fair they come from different backgrounds, it's not like it's a student campus or a hippy thing; similarly, it's not a sink estate or a football hooligan type of affair either. It seems to be a lot of different people from different walks of life; however, I've observed over the past 12-18 months they do have a lot of common traits when doing their ranting. One of them the making of vague and fairly unobservable claims and also relying heavily on anecdotes, personal experiences and testimonials. This makes all of their claims difficult to disprove.

One of the other traits of this angry mob is cherry picking information confirming some evidence but ignoring and minimizing disconfirming evidence; this is mixed with what has been described in recent years by technobabble, basically words that sound scientific but if you check them out make no sense. This is normally lost on the warrior putting it up on their social media page because it's invariably cut and pasted.

They also profess certainty and talk of 'proof' with great

confidence. It's back to the old FACT friend after every sentence and in this rapidly changing attitude toward this unique era with a pandemic we all know little about is unchanging and doesn't self-correct or progress despite moderate people doing exactly that as we pick up a bit of knowledge about the condition caused by the virus.

I've also been alerted to the fact that anti-vaxxers commit logical fallacies, their arguments contain many elementary errors in reasoning and it all lacks peer review going directly to the public avoiding scientific scrutiny. Finally, there's always an alleged conspiracy to suppress their ideas that there's 'people out there wanting to get this show banned' going back to an earlier observation.

There are two quotes that sum up this kind of wilful ignorance and sum up a lot of part wilful part deluded part lazy reasons why I wrote this book; and the first one is this from Thomas Sowell:

'The reason so many people misunderstand so many issues is not that these issues are so complex, but that people do not want a factual or analytical explanation that leaves them emotionally unsatisfied.'

Politicians of both main parties tap into this all the time and try to appeal to the over emotional, to the simple thinkers and the romantics that see some civil servant not as they should be but as some hero riding in on their white charger to save them. As has been touched on earlier, people love 'plain speakers' or people who 'tell it like it is', but can't see past the fact that these straight talkers might be straight talking a pile of shite. The other great quote is this one:

'In an anti-intellectual society, people who know nothing about a complex subject are emboldened to ridicule experts who have spent a lifetime studying it.'

That to me is the embodiment of this book and is from George Kiser who believe it or not is a billionaire businessman who has been listed as one of the top 50 philanthropists and has reported to have given half his fortune away.

I'm just a stand-up comic and I deal mainly in jokes and trying to make people laugh, which I said at the beginning of the book. However, if you can take something from this book it's this. Read a few books and watch a few documentaries and then always follow news stories on a particular subject. Then when someone starts spouting on said subject just politely drop your reasoned and balanced views on the subject. If that someone begins ridiculing you, then they're the fuckwit, not you. Yes, it's a rule of thumb, but it's a good rule of thumb.

AND FINALLY WHAT
OF BUDDHISM?

Well as you know this is not what the book is about, it's a MacGuffin as they say. Buddhism is only one example of the many big subjects people cover to talk freely of their supposed knowledge on stuff they know nowt about.

My quick answer to this is surely, I don't know, it's an enormous topic I couldn't possibly say; however, in the spirit of this book I'll chuck an opinion out there despite the fact I don't really know the first thing about it.

Rather like acupuncture, it seems to work. The inner peace and the meditation seems to put people at peace. Lots of people travel to the Buddhist parts of the world (I'm deliberately making this a bit moronic) to practise it. It must have something. Myself though? Nah not for me. It all looks a bit mental. I couldn't take the rubbish clothes or the shaving of my head. The food doesn't appeal to me either, there's no pie and chips in Buddhist circles or beef Sunday dinner. By the way I'm not a philistine with union jack blinkers, there's no hot mezze or kebabs in the Lebanese or Greek style, no enchiladas or lasagne. Too much commitment to the cause as well. I might have to show some discipline or give up on a night out or a lie in or something! It also seems humourless and lacking in a sense of irony or self-parody. There seems to be no gallows humour, just smart arsed proverbs proving why Buddhists know fucking best about everything. Lots of wankers seem to like it as well, which is a good rule of thumb to not like a thing.

When I was working in Singapore, a taxi driver asked if I'd like to visit the local Buddhist temple the next morning. The person I was working with was a pain in the arse and was in said taxi as well. She was well up for it and said that she'd give me a knock the next morning. I pretended I was asleep and claimed that I didn't hear her knocking when we were at the gig the following night. Whether it was because I couldn't be arsed with her company, or I genuinely couldn't be bothered to go to a Buddhist temple that was practically next door because I'm a lazy westerner, I don't know. What I do know is that it's not for me and although I'm sure it's great being a Buddhist I can tell you it's great being an old punk as well, the only difference being that I don't feel the need to tell all and sundry that they must listen to The Angelic Upstarts and it might change their life. The white middle class, you know the ones that are kind of part time Buddhists, do espouse the Buddhist way whenever you meet them like they're on some kind of divine commission.

So, to give a nod to all the morons: Buddhism, load of rubbish! Thank you and goodnight.